contents

iv

CHARACTER MAP

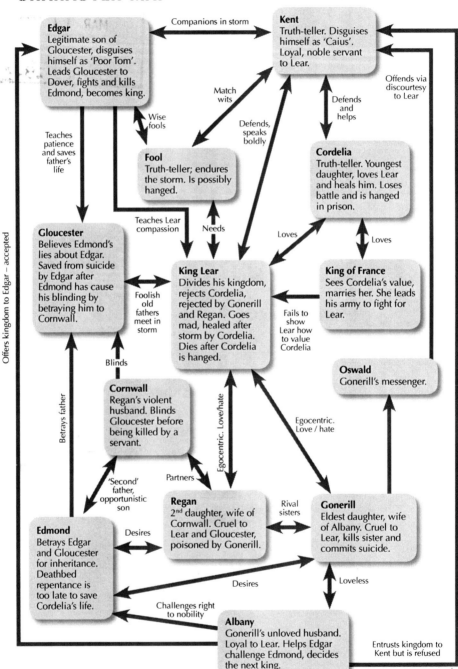

Insight Study Guide
Sue Tweg

King Lear

William Shakespeare

insight

insight

William Shakespeare's King Lear by Sue Tweg
Insight Study Guide series

Copyright © 2011 Insight Publications Pty Ltd

First published in 2010,
reprinted in 2011 by
Insight Publications Pty Ltd
ABN 57 005 102 983
89 Wellington Street
St Kilda VIC 3182
Australia
Tel: +61 3 9523 0044
Fax: +61 3 9523 2044
Email: books@insightpublications.com
Website: www.insightpublications.com

This edition published 2011 in the United States of America by
Insight Publications Pty Ltd, Australia.

ISBN-13: 978-1-921411-63-2

Library of Congress Control Number: 2011931335

Cover Design by The Modern Art Production Group
Cover Illustrations by The Modern Art Production Group,
istockphoto® and House Industries
Internal Design by Sarn Potter

Printed in the United States of America by Lightning Source
10 9 8 7 6 5 4 3 2 1

OVERVIEW

About the play and its author

Jan Kott, the modern European writer and director, provocatively wrote that 'King Lear gives one the impression of a high mountain that everyone admires, yet no one particularly wishes to climb' (Shakespeare Our Contemporary, 1965, p.100). He wrote that, at least in the 1960s, it was as though this play were out of place in modern theatre. This guide is designed to help you to climb that daunting mountain and glimpse for yourself a remarkable view of your own from the top. Very few people could claim that they really grasp the whole meaning of this great play. Nevertheless, it has plenty of ideas to stimulate our thinking about today's world: it repays close study and is wonderful to encounter as a text for performance.

The old story of King Lear (usually spelt Leir in sources) and his three daughters was well known to Shakespeare's audiences in ballads, tales and prose histories such as Shakespeare's favourite source, Holinshed's Chronicle (1587). Between late 1603 and 1605 (when an older Leir play, which Shakespeare would certainly have known, was published), Shakespeare reworked this material and combined it with other strands of character and plot from Sir Philip Sidney's prose romance Arcadia (1590), along with a recently published document by Samuel Harsnett (see below) to shape a powerful new tragedy. It was performed by the King's Men at the Globe theatre, possibly in 1605 but certainly in 1606 and was chosen later that year to be presented at Court before the new king, James I, as part of the Christmas entertainments.

As well as an anonymous publication of the Leir story, a number of contemporary events may also have suggested the topicality of a Lear play to Shakespeare. There was residual social anxiety surrounding the accession of James Stuart to the English throne following Elizabeth I's death in 1603. Old religious differences surfaced in reports of bogus exorcisms. Families battled over disputed inheritances. As it turned out, Shakespeare's company benefited by James' accession. They came under royal patronage as the newly titled King's Men, and featured in his coronation procession.

King Lear as we know it is a mature Shakespearean tragedy with powerful and enduring themes. Ideas such as loss of power, old age, family rivalries, madness, the duties of rulers, blindness in all its forms, the mysteries of human nature and questions about the meaning of life in a frighteningly unknowable cosmos make up the complex and challenging fabric of the play. Audiences find it emotionally overwhelming. Actors, too, need to be psychologically mature enough and have physical stamina to undertake the main roles of Lear, Gloucester and Edgar.

Shakespeare's plays have attracted commentary from students, critics, scholars and theatre practitioners across the centuries. Dr Johnson, writing as a Georgian editor of Shakespeare's plays, viewed *King Lear* as exceptional because every scene 'agitates our passions and interests our curiosity' but complained that Gloucester's onstage blinding was 'an act too horrid to be endured in dramatick [sic] exhibition'. He also found it hard to tolerate the injustice of the ending: 'A play in which the wicked prosper, and the virtuous miscarry, may doubtless be good, because it is a just representation of the common events of human life', although the audience would be 'better pleased from the final triumph of persecuted virtue' (*Preface to King Lear*, 1765).

Johnson writes with reference to Shakespeare's text but we need to remember that theatregoers in the 18th century would have preferred Nahum Tate's 1681 adaptation of *King Lear*, which omitted the Fool and provided a romantic ending, with Lear alive and Cordelia as Edgar's happy bride. Read Halio's Introduction (pp.32–51) for an excellent comprehensive survey of the play's performance history as Shakespeare's text was gradually restored. Johnson's view of the play has been shared by many other critics and practitioners, trying to make sense of a brilliant but bleak vision of human life.

Synopsis

The action has been divided into **Main plot** and **Sub-plot** in this guide to make the developing lines within the two family groups clearer for study. From the opening scene the two plots are interwoven and complementary. **Act 1 Main plot:** Having decided to relinquish his responsibilities as King of Britain (without giving up any royal privileges), Lear devises a rhetorical love test for his three daughters, Gonerill, Regan and Cordelia. Their share of the kingdom will be dependent on how well they individually please their father in flattering speeches. Cordelia, Lear's acknowledged favourite, refuses to participate and is banished, as is the loyal courtier the Earl of Kent, who challenges Lear's faulty judgment. Cordelia becomes the wife of the King of France and leaves the country, distrustful that her elder sisters will care properly for their elderly father. Regan and Gonerill discuss how to manage their father's unruliness. Kent returns, in disguise, to serve Lear. Gonerill rejects her father and he curses her, beginning to feel madness rising within him.

Act 1 Sub-plot: Lear's courtier, the Earl of Gloucester, is manipulated by his illegitimate son Edmond to suspect his legitimate heir, Edgar, of treachery.

Act 2 Main plot: Cornwall and Regan leave home to avoid having to entertain Lear, and go to Gloucester's castle to meet Gonerill. Kent attacks Gonerill's servant Oswald and is punished by being put in the stocks. Lear and Gloucester meet and commiserate. Gonerill and Regan strip Lear of all his retainers and push him out into the gathering storm at night with only Kent and the Fool for company.

Act 2 Sub-plot: Edmond stages a mock fight to help Edgar escape from their father. Edgar takes on the disguise of 'Poor Tom' to survive.

Act 3 Main plot: Lear succumbs to madness on the heath in a storm. Kent and the Fool accompany him. They meet 'Poor Tom' and shelter together in a hovel before being helped by Gloucester.

Act 3 Sub-plot: Gloucester confides in Edmond that he's in contact with Cordelia's army in Dover. Edmond denounces him as a traitor to Cornwall, who confers Gloucester's title on him. After helping Lear, Gloucester is blinded by Cornwall and cast out of his home.

Act 4 Main plot: Gonerill woos Edmond and plots her husband Albany's death. Cordelia searches for Lear, to heal and comfort him. Lear and Gloucester meet after the latter's suicide attempt.

Act 4 Sub-plot: Edgar as 'Tom' meets Gloucester and agrees to lead him to Dover. Gloucester tries to commit suicide but is prevented by Edgar, who begins to teach patience in suffering to his father. Edgar kills Oswald to protect his father and finds Gonerill's letter to Edmond. The battle begins.

Act 5 Main plot: Cordelia and Lear are captured and sent to prison under Edmond's orders to be killed. Kent asks for Lear, too late. Lear enters with the dead Cordelia in his arms, then dies of grief. Edgar becomes Britain's new ruler.

Act 5 Sub-plot: Edgar gives Albany Gonerill's treacherous letter and asks for a duel with Edmond at the right moment. Albany agrees. Edgar mortally wounds Edmond, who attempts to rescind the order for Lear's and Cordelia's deaths, too late. Edmond, Gonerill and Regan are all laid together in death.

Character summaries

(Named characters only. Minor roles are discussed in the relevant scene notes.)

Lear, King of Britain: Aged about 80, Lear foolishly divides his kingdom between his daughters and is driven mad by their cruelty. He is rescued by Cordelia but is captured in battle and dies of grief when Cordelia is hanged.

Gonerill: Lear's eldest daughter, tough-minded and murderous. She's cursed by her father for refusing to maintain him and his hundred knights. Gonerill is married to Albany but loves Edmond. She kills herself when confronted with her incriminating letter.

Regan: Lear's second daughter, outwardly gentle and 'feminine' in her treatment of Lear. Married to Cornwall, she's revealed to be equally sadistic in her cruelty to Gloucester. She also denies Lear his followers and shelter from the storm. Gonerill poisons Regan because the sisters are rivals for Edmond's love.

Cordelia: Lear's youngest daughter, who says 'nothing' to flatter Lear and is banished. She marries the King of France, returning with an army to fight her sisters and rescue Lear. She is captured with Lear and hanged in prison on Edmond's orders.

The King of France: Cordelia's chivalrous husband. He chooses to marry Cordelia for her virtues even though she has been disinherited by Lear, and offers his country's army to restore Lear as king.

The Duke of Burgundy: France's rival suitor for Cordelia. He immediately rejects Cordelia as a potential wife when Lear disowns her and her dowry vanishes.

The Duke of Albany: Gonerill's husband. He criticises her for mistreating Lear and never goes along wholeheartedly with her plans for war against Cordelia and Lear. A senior nobleman and a survivor of the tragedy, he nominates Edgar as Britain's new king.

The Duke of Cornwall: Regan's husband, an angry, cruel bully who is very conscious of his own power. He's mortally wounded by a servant while he's blinding Gloucester. When he dies, he's replaced by Edmond in Regan's plans.

The Earl of Gloucester: An old nobleman. His role is comparable with Lear's, as another foolish father deceived by a child. Gloucester's mistake is to trust his illegitimate son, Edmond, and suspect his loyal son, Edgar, of plotting against his life. He is blinded by Cornwall for aiding Lear and then attempts suicide at Dover but is comforted by Edgar, who ensures his safety until his death.

Edgar: Gloucester's legitimate son and heir, aged in his mid 20s. He trusts Edmond, who counsels him to run for his life. Disguised as 'Poor Tom', a mad beggar, Edgar shelters in the hovel with Lear, Kent and the Fool, then joins his blind father as a protective guide to Dover. Still unidentified, he challenges Edmond to a duel and wins, then hands Albany Gonerill's letter which reveals her treachery. He survives to become king after Lear's death.

Edmond: Gloucester's illegitimate son and half-brother to Edgar, Edmond is a clever, plausible, amoral villain, encouraging the sexual interest of Gonerill and Regan. Because he controls the action after the battle, Lear and Cordelia fall into his power. His motivation in condemning them is to inherit the kingdom. A final duel reveals Edmond's treachery. His sudden desire to do 'some good' before he dies fails to save Cordelia's life.

The Earl of Kent: Banished by Lear for defending Cordelia, Kent is a loyal subject who follows Lear through to the end, disguised as 'Caius'. Although offered the crown by Albany at the end, Kent refuses, preferring to follow his master Lear to his death.

The Fool: Lear's servant companion, characterised as a daring, sad, wise and witty speaker of truths from 1.4 to 3.6, after which he inexplicably disappears. His closeness to Cordelia is notable – when she is banished the Fool pines away. At the end, Lear comments that his 'poor fool is hanged', although it is uncertain whether he's referring to Cordelia or the Fool himself.

Oswald: Gonerill's foppish steward and possible lover (by inference). He carries messages between the sisters. Following Regan's hint, Oswald tries to kill Gloucester when he finds him but Edgar kills him instead. His last act is to pass on Gonerill's incriminating letter to Edgar.

Curan: A servant of Gloucester's who appears in one scene with Edmond (2.1), to pass on gossip and the latest news about possible war between Albany and Cornwall. His brief speeches set the tone of instability between apparent allies.

BACKGROUND & CONTEXT

The circumstances under which Shakespeare wrote his play and how it related to another recently printed but decade-old anonymous play *King Leir and his three daughters,* (recorded for publication in the Stationers' Register in 1605) are unknown. Some theatre rivalry or text piracy was possibly involved, because another entry in the Stationers' Register for 26 November 1607 specifies 'A booke called Master William Shakespeare his historye of Kinge Lear as yt was played before the Kinges Majestie at Whitehall upon Sainct Stephens night at Christmas Last, by his majesties servantes playing usually at the Globe on the Bancksyde' (in Bullough, VII, pp.269).

This stage work, however popular with audiences, would have had only a few showings at the Globe when it was new. There was no such thing as a run of several weeks. *King Lear* probably had a few scattered days' playing with occasional repeats such as the Christmas showing at Court.

While you should be aware that Shakespeare's play exists in printed Quarto (Q) and Folio (F) versions, some significant variations between texts are problematic to editors and text scholars. However, most scholars nowadays consider the Folio text to be Shakespeare's own revision of his earlier Quarto text.

1603: A year of significant events

Although it isn't always possible (or even wise) to spend time tracing likely sources or contemporary historical references for a work of fiction, the case is slightly different with Shakespeare, whose plays habitually borrow from existing literary works and contain topical references of interest to his audiences. Borrowings in the case of *King Lear* give us insight into the complex fabric of ideas and images in the play.

A new king: unification of the kingdom

The issue of a divided kingdom, central to the *Lear* story, was a subject of hot debate around this time. Although Queen Elizabeth had delayed naming her heir, and a flurry of plots were uncovered in 1603, 1604 and 1605 (the infamous 'Gunpowder' plot), England passed relatively smoothly into the hands of James VI of Scotland. James made it known that he wanted to unify the two kingdoms. Despite serious parliamentary opposition, a form of agreement was reached in 1608, to the extent that all subjects born after 1603 were recognised to have a common nationality.

James I's plan to unify the crowns of England and Scotland, together with his autocratic ideas about power derived from God, combined to reawaken questions about royal prerogative that had been raised in Elizabeth's reign. Ancient precedents informed these conversations: the *Leir* stories of a divided kingdom and civil war belonged to what was known as 'The Matter of Britain', a collection of chronicle histories about ancient Britain's invaders, rulers (including Leir or Ina) and heroes. Look for extracts from Geoffrey of Monmouth, Holinshed, Harrison and Camden (in Bullough VII, pp.311–22). Some productions and films of *King Lear* reference these quasi-mythical times by including Stonehenge sets and Druids.

Dealing with elderly parents: the Annesley case

In 1603, the case of old Bryan Annesley and his daughters (Grace, Christian and Cordell) came to public attention. This was the most recent of a series of court cases from the late Elizabethan period where the question of a disputed inheritance, complicated by parental incapacity, was the issue. Annesley, who had been a minor courtier to Elizabeth I, was a wealthy old 'Gentleman Pensioner' from Kent. Two of his daughters were married but the third, Cordell, looked after him at home because he was frail. His eldest daughter Grace and her husband, Sir John Wildgose, tried but failed to have Bryan declared a senile and incompetent lunatic. Cordell wrote letters to Robert Cecil, the Lord Treasurer, and argued passionately to defend her father's dignity. The court defended her appeals and she became the main beneficiary when he died in 1604.

There's no evidence that Shakespeare knew more about the case than he could have picked up through gossip, although the name 'Cordell' must have struck a chord with 'Cordella' [sic] in the old play. The case may well have sparked enough interest to warrant printing the older *Leir* play, which in turn prompted Shakespeare. The issue itself – family squabbles over money coupled with the problem of ageing parents – cannot have been unusual, then as now, and provided plenty of food for thought as material for tragedy.

(The letters relating to this case can be found in Bullough, VII, pp.309–11.)

Disturbed states of mind

King Lear foregrounds two fundamentally significant and interrelated social terrors of Shakespeare's time: fear of poverty and mental instability. The lives of people with disturbed psychological states in Shakespeare's England were not enviable. Discussion of the range of mental conditions had not advanced much beyond the mediaeval formulation of Humours, which could make quite subtle theoretical distinctions between moods or habitual personality traits (Choleric, Sanguine, Phlegmatic or Melancholic) but could do little either practically or with herbal medication to assist a person undergoing a severe nervous breakdown, as Lear is shown to do. Commonly cited causes of madness were melancholia (the kind of depressed grief Gloucester feels), hysteria (*hysterica passio* or 'the mother', described precisely as that by Lear in 2.4.52–3), or demonic possession (which Edgar pretends to suffer as part of his 'Poor Tom' disguise).

If they could not be looked after at home, the insane were locked up in local 'houses of correction' that included Bedlam, the short name for the Hospital of St Mary of Bethlehem in London, used since 1547 as an asylum. It must have been more like a holding pen than a hospital: if inmates hadn't recovered in a year they were simply discharged into the community.

When Bedlam inmates were free they often joined other vagrants to wander the countryside. Elizabethan Vagrancy Laws were severe: homeless offenders could be whipped out of a town, taken back to their home parish and whipped there or punished with a day or night in the stocks (like Kent). 'Poor Tom' was the generic name for more-or-less deranged vagrants in Shakespeare's day, who tried (if they could) to beg for their basic needs.

Deranged wanderers by default were the poorest of the poor (something King Lear begins to understand during his time on the heath). By the terms of the Poor Law, each parish was responsible for supporting its own needy souls but no others. Despite Christian teaching about charity, begging was frowned upon and almsgiving was not encouraged.

Shakespeare was aware of this reality. He also knew the contents of a book by Samuel Harsnett, published in 1603, that focused on the expression of (pretended) madness brought about by (supposedly) diabolic possession. He crafted Edgar's speeches and antics as 'Poor Tom' by borrowing directly from Harsnett's *Declaration of Egregious* [flagrant] *Popish Impostures*. The fiercely anti-Catholic Harsnett was Chaplain to the Anglican Bishop of London when he presented his report, commissioned by the Privy Council, exposing cases of fraudulent possession and bogus 'exorcisms' orchestrated by Jesuits to make converts to Rome. Harsnett documented raving speeches so precisely that Shakespeare could colour Edgar's masterly performance with genuine names and phrases. (If you are interested, find Harsnett extracts in Bullough, VII, pp.414–20 and Kenneth Muir's list of matches in his Arden edition of *King Lear*, 1964, pp.253–6.)

Another significant publication of 1603, by a Dr Edward Jorden, was entitled *A Briefe Discourse of a Disease called the Suffocation of the Mother*. Like Harsnett and many others sceptical about charges of witchcraft against innocent people and cases of 'demonic possession', Jorden recognised the urgent need to protect people with hysteria from being victimised or exploited. His book was an early account of psychosomatic illness and urged people to look for natural causes before reaching for supernatural ones. Jorden's work cannot be matched as a source for *King Lear* as directly as Harsnett's but his observations are pertinent to the range of disorders Shakespeare describes.

Theatre as a metaphor for life

> When we are born, we cry that we are come/ To this great stage of fools (Lear, 4.5.174–5)

Lear's meditation on the world as a stage is characteristic of Shakespeare's times. Short poems by contemporaries (including Spenser and Sir Walter Raleigh) make the same point – look up an especially poignant poem attributed to Raleigh, beginning 'What is our life? A play of passion'.

'All the world's a stage' was a well-known tag centuries before Shakespeare's character Jaques started a famous speech with it in 1599 (*As You Like It*, 2.7.139–66). The same image informs action and ideas in *Hamlet* and *Macbeth*. *King Lear* is full of theatre metaphors about life as a series of roles (like king, fool, beggar, loyal son, loving daughter) and disguises (Kent, Edgar), playing and deception (Gonerill, Regan, Edmond).

GENRE, STRUCTURE & LANGUAGE

Genre

Tragedy

If you are familiar with any classical Greek tragedies, you'll notice similarities with *King Lear* in the kinds of questions posed by those plays. Sophocles and Euripides present flawed or unaware characters who are inadvertently caught in traps of their own making and undergo cruel tests, without ever fully understanding how they could have avoided the terrible outcome. The Olympian gods are constantly invoked in these plays but remain aloof, apparently unconcerned with human suffering. Aristotle's formulation of rules for tragedy continues to dominate our interpretation of the genre, but remember that he was neither a dramatist nor lived at the time of Greece's greatest playwrights.

Shakespearean tragedy

King Lear follows Aristotelian patterning in that it has a coherent plot that shows the fall of noble persons, brought about by a tragic flaw or weakness of character. Characters, who are neither all good nor all bad, move from a state of *hubris* (the highest state of pride and certainty) to experience tragic reversal of fortune, then moments of crisis, recognition and revelation, after which the final catastrophe occurs to end the play. Audience members experience strong feelings of pity and terror, which Aristotle defined sketchily in the term *catharsis*. So Lear and Gloucester are each brought down by a tragic flaw, then redeemed, then brought down again by external forces. By the end, the audience is as stunned as Edgar, whose final lines struggle to make any sense of 'this sad time' (5.3.298).

Shakespeare characteristically binds classical patterns to mediaeval and renaissance humanistic thinking. He combines images of Olympian gods, Fortune's wheel and contemporary philosophical ideas in a dramatically rich dialogue about the perennial tragic pattern of rise and fall, prosperity and decay, power and loss for *all* living things. See the **Themes** section below for further discussion.

Theatre of cruelty

Ideas about the absurdity of life, especially in Europe after the Second World War, led to several strong restatements of what theatre could show and tell. Antonin Artaud wrote that 'Without an element of cruelty at the root of every spectacle, the theatre is not possible'. Edward Bond's 1971 play, Lear, is a comparatively recent example of the genre which has been influenced by Jan Kott and Peter Brook.

Historical drama

Prose histories of Britain such as Holinshed's Chronicles provided source material for many playwrights, including Shakespeare. In its subject matter, King Lear can be bracketed with plays such as Cymbeline, Hengist, Gorboduc and Locrine. General interest in these remote kings was real, linking contemporary political discussion to genuine antiquarian curiosity about Britain's semi-legendary past. Find a copy of John Speed's map of Saxon England and look at the border illustrations. Speed's Atlas (1616) was part of a grand scheme to write a history of Britain from the Roman Conquest to the accession of James I and, of course, was dedicated to the King.

Structure

This edition of the play is divided into five Acts, each subdivided into scenes and notated thus: 1.1 (denotes Act 1 scene 1), 4.3 (denotes Act 4 scene 3). You should insert line details in brackets after quoting, e.g. (4.3.27–8), when you illustrate a point in an essay.

Structurally, the play charts the destructive consequences of two acts of folly committed by two old men, Lear and Gloucester, who are leaders of society and fathers. By their actions in Act 1 they lose control and break family bonds, which forces them both to take painful physical and emotional journeys into the wild natural world of experience in Acts 2, 3 and 4. The play follows them both through madness and torture to some enlightenment at the end of their lives in Act 5, when they are finally reconciled with the children they rejected. Although the two plot lines initially evolve along parallel tracks, they are thematically linked and characters converge as the storm begins (end of Act 2).

Note: In an interview with J Meadowcroft, Donald Sinden (an actor who played Lear) commented on the way 1.1 of King Lear feels like the last scene of another play. It's as though the action is almost over, courtiers wait for the will to be read, the kingdom is divided and the king prepares to die. Then, out of Cordelia's 'Nothing', the play suddenly ignites into violent action. Sinden's interview can be found in 'Playing King Lear', *Shakespeare Survey* 33 1980, pp.81–7 (with production photos).

Time

The unfolding action of the play can't be measured day by day but is imagined to take place over a period of weeks or months. The tragedy is so intense that it seems to compress time and space into a single catastrophic moment.

Place

The geographical setting is unclear but Shakespeare creates a sense of tired and starving people moving rapidly up and down the country in feverish activity – notice how little stillness there is in the play. After the events of 1.1, Cordelia travels from Lear's palace (in the Midlands; possibly Leicester) to France. Sometime later she returns to Britain with an army. Gonerill and Regan go home with their husbands (most likely to Cornwall and Northumbria), then communicate by letters and meet up at Gloucester's house (presumably in Gloucester), where Kent and Lear also meet again. The action moves down to Dover on the South coast for the battle. The frequent exchanges of letters indicate where people are and how they keep informed of events.

Language

Shakespeare mixes the rhythms of poetic speech (blank verse in iambic pentameter) with prose, with the occasional use of doggerel rhyming verse from the Fool. Shakespeare's English can be challenging for modern readers. Professional actors work hard to understand the language, how to stress words or colour their tone to give meaning to speeches. Below are a few pointers.

Blank verse

Non-rhyming lines of poetry indicate a more formal mode of speech than prose. Feel the iambic pentameter pulse as you emphasise five syllables in each ten syllable line. Don't stop at the end of a line if there's no punctuation – just follow the sense of the words. Iambic pentameter shouldn't sound mechanical or singsong but approximates formal English speech.

Notice how often in this play an extra syllable or two creeps into the lines. Poetry and prose rhythms are coming together, as in Lear's opening line which has eleven syllables. Try reading Gonerill and Regan's set-piece speeches in 1.1 for some examples of 'bumpy' rhythms underneath smooth sentiments.

Sometimes the reverse happens. Some lines are short by one or more syllables – think about why Shakespeare has used silent beats instead of words. What is the character expressing by not speaking in these instances? Compare Cordelia's 'Nothing, my lord' (1.1.82) and Edmond's 'Nothing, my lord' (1.2.31). Are they saying the same thing? In the same way?

Prose

Unlike other Shakespeare plays where prose dialogue is often reserved for common vernacular or comic interludes, prose is spoken at times by most characters in *King Lear*. The play opens with Gloucester and Kent speaking prose, and Gonerill and Regan lapse into prose to express the urgency of the moment after Cordelia leaves in 1.1. Gloucester even points out the alteration in 'Poor Tom's' voice as they shift from prose into blank verse in 4.5. Lear's madness, too, is expressed in both prose and verse. The language mix gives this tragedy a particularly human dimension and brings it closer to the audience.

Thou and you

Look carefully at how characters in the play address each other directly. Modern English has lost the distinctive informal second-person pronoun, but it was a significant marker in Shakespeare's time (just as it still is in European languages). The formal 'you' is polite address. Depending on context, the informal 'thou' can insult the person being addressed (by indicating lower status than the speaker, or contempt and belittlement), or indicate familiarity. In Edgar's line, 'O **thou** side-piercing sight' (4.5.84), 'thou' signals the strength of his pity for Lear.

Imagery

Shakespeare's language is metaphorical, full of ideas expressed in images that need some thought to picture and understand. What does Lear mean when he says he is 'bound upon a wheel of fire'? Why does he call Gonerill and Regan 'these pelican daughters'? Be alert to imagery relating to the play's main themes: cosmic influence (relating to gods, heaven and the supernatural), madness, eyes and 'seeing', and nature. Highlight or note examples of imagery in the text margin.

Soliloquies

Pay attention to Edmond's prose soliloquy in 1.2, Kent's short justification at the beginning of 1.4, and Edgar's description of his transformation into 'Poor Tom' in 2.3. After Edmond's Machiavellian invocation to Nature to help his intrigues to succeed in 1.2, Lear's address to the storm in 3.2 is the nearest thing to a formal soliloquy (and even that is interrupted by the Fool). None of these soliloquies resemble the poetic set-pieces of Shakespeare's other tragedies, yet they all mark important moments and communicate a character's thoughts to the audience.

SCENE-BY-SCENE ANALYSIS

Note: Every scene contributes to the thematic complexity of this intense play. Nonetheless, quite a few **key scenes** have been singled out for careful study, either because they contain interactions that are crucial to understanding a character or because they contain significant wordplay. Take special care in analysing these scenes: they can form the basis for class discussions, reading aloud and essay work.

Act 1

1.1
Summary: Lear divides his kingdom according to which daughter claims to love him the most.

Key Scene

This long opening scene, usually known as the 'map' scene, introduces two plot strands involving divided families. Shakespeare introduces an uneasy sense of the natural order (and the political state) being turned upside down, forming the core structure of the tragedy to come. The action evolves in four steps:

- Gloucester makes crude comments to Kent about his bastard son, Edmond (in Edmond's presence).
- Lear demonstrates how he intends to divide his kingdom: his decision to award territory demands a public demonstration of his daughters' love. Gonerill and Regan play their father's game as he expects them to – they flatter him

excessively and are granted large portions of the kingdom. Cordelia refuses to speak her love.

- Cordelia is banished by Lear but offered marriage by the King of France, who recognises her worth. Kent is banished for criticising Lear and defending Cordelia.
- Cordelia leaves for France, warning her sisters to 'Love our father well' (1.1.265). Left alone, Gonerill and Regan make plans to control Lear.

Q What qualities differentiate Cordelia's two suitors? How do they represent two opposing sets of values?

1.2

Summary: *Edmond schemes to inherit his father's land.*

The subplot begins. Edmond can't inherit because he's illegitimate but plans to take Edgar's land anyway. He fools his father with lies implicating his half-brother, Edgar. Gloucester's general anxiety about the times makes him susceptible. Edmond finds Edgar equally gullible because he's 'noble' and full of 'foolish honesty'; we notice his double entendre after Edgar's puzzled 'Some villain hath done me wrong' (1.2.138).

Q How have the events of the previous scene contributed to Gloucester's state of mind in 1.2?

1.3

Summary: *Lear has begun his new life.*

At Gonerill's house, Lear is putting into practice his plan to stay with his daughters and enjoy life. His already diminishing status is signalled by Gonerill's irritated response to Lear's Fool and 'riotous' knights, and by her instruction to Oswald (her steward) to put on 'what weary negligence you please' (1.3.13).

Q Does Gonerill have some cause to be critical of Lear's behaviour?

1.4

Summary: *Kent returns in disguise to serve Lear.*

KEY SCENE

Kent (disguised as a gentleman named 'Caius') rejoins Lear and tries to reassert his master's dignity by tripping up Oswald, who is acting disrespectfully as instructed by Gonerill. Even one of Lear's knights notices the change of mood, 'a great abatement of kindness' (1.4.51). Lear's Fool enters the play. Lear curses Gonerill.

Q How does the Fool change the atmosphere in the scene?

Q How do you think Gonerill would react to Lear's dreadful curse? View the scene in Brook's film – tears run down her cheeks.

1.5
Summary: The Fool mocks Lear.

KEY SCENE

The Fool verbally chastises Lear (who fears he's going mad after Gonerill's rejection). Pay attention to the Fool's clever yet serious wordplay about crab-apples.

Q Why does the Fool (who is often beaten) suggest that Lear needs to be beaten?

2.1
Summary: Edmond continues his ploy.

The subplot develops. Edmond tricks Edgar into engaging in a mock fight to avoid a meeting with his father. Gloucester again falls for Edmond's hypocritical incrimination of Edgar (including a forged letter as 'evidence') and sends men to hunt him down. Cornwall and Regan, who sympathise with Edmond's show of filial loyalty, are welcomed to Gloucester's house.

Q Why does Regan make so much of the fact that Edgar is Lear's godson?

2.2
Summary: Kent is set in the stocks.

Kent attacks Oswald again, for which Cornwall insists he must be punished. Gloucester commiserates with Kent but is anxious not to oppose Cornwall. Kent is sentenced to be put in the stocks, a crude wooden frame that traps a person by the legs in a sitting position. People could throw stones or rotten food at the unfortunate person and serious injury could result. Kent is left out in the cold overnight. Alone in the moonlight, he reads a letter from Cordelia, who knows of Lear's ill-treatment.

Q How does Oswald attempt to defend himself from Kent's accusations?

2.3

Summary: *Edgar disguises himself.*

KEY SCENE

Knowing that he's hunted as a traitor, Edgar desperately chooses a disguise that is the reverse of his normal personality. As a 'Bedlam beggar' he will be completely unrecognisable – and his emotional distress can find an outlet in 'Poor Tom's' gibberish. Edgar changes his outer appearance and practises a different way of speaking.

Q What will Edgar's disguise expose him to and teach him?

2.4

Summary: *Kent is freed from the stocks ahead of the developing storm.*

KEY SCENE

This scene evolves in four dramatic steps:

- Lear and the Fool come across Kent in the stocks. The Fool again uses pointed wordplay.
- Gloucester tries unsuccessfully to quell Lear's rage against his disobedient daughters. The Fool exacerbates Lear's shattered sense of authority.
- Regan confronts Lear diplomatically. Lear still believes she is gentle but, when Gonerill arrives, the sisters break Lear by working together in a cruelly synchronised verbal strategy.
- Lear makes an impassioned speech about 'need' (2.4.257–79) before rushing away into the night (with Kent and the Fool following) as a storm begins. Cornwall and Regan order Gloucester to shut his doors against Lear.

Q How has the information communicated through letters contributed to the drama of this scene? See Kent's speech (lines 2.4.24–42).

3.1

Summary: *Kent seeks out Lear.*

Kent tells the audience that Albany and Cornwall are not natural allies in the coming war. He asks a Gentleman to look out for Cordelia, who will be coming from France to rescue her father.

Q What is the purpose of this brief scene? Could it be omitted without losing anything of importance to the play?

3.2

Summary: *Lear encourages the storm.*

KEY SCENE

Lear contributes to the conjuring up of the storm by imbuing it with symbolic retributive force. The Fool, cold and desperate, makes comments about houses and women. Kent helps them find shelter in a nearby hovel [an old shack].

Q What lessons about life are to be learnt in the storm?

3.3

Summary: *Edmond again furthers his plot.*

Gloucester confides in Edmond that he dislikes being ordered about in his own house by Cornwall: he's in secret communication with Cordelia's invading army. When Gloucester goes out into the storm to help Lear, Edmond decides to betray his father to Cornwall and steal his title.

Q What will be the immediate consequences of Gloucester's actions?

3.4

Summary: *Lear's madness becomes increasingly evident as the storm rages on.*

KEY SCENE

(Continuation of 3.2) The storm continues through the night, both in the natural world and within Lear's crazed mind. The Fool is frightened by 'Poor Tom' who has been sheltering in the hovel. Gloucester, not recognising his son or Kent, conducts them all to food and shelter.

Q What insight does Lear gain in this scene when he reflects on his own condition and the way other people live in the world?

Q Why do you think the Fool becomes so quiet when 'Poor Tom' begins to speak?

3.5

Summary: *Edmond's scheme against his father is complete.*

Cornwall rewards Edmond for betraying his father, the 'traitor' Gloucester. Their conversation shows them to be a pair of hypocrites. Cornwall (the sadistic bully) moralises that Edgar's 'evil disposition' is only to be expected, a natural consequence of his father's 'reprovable badness'

(3.5.6). Edmond hypocritically bewails his 'malicious fortune' that makes him feel bad about doing the right thing in betraying a traitor.

Q Is Cornwall a more appropriate 'father' for Edmond than Gloucester?

3.6

Summary: *It becomes apparent that Lear's life is under threat.*

(Continuation of 3.4) The Fool and Edgar engage with Lear's deranged state of mind, while Kent stands guard. Gloucester finds out that Lear's life is in imminent danger and determines he must be taken to Dover. Edgar is so distressed he can barely stay in character. This scene is the Fool's last appearance.

Q Why is Kent's comment to Gloucester, 'The gods reward your kindness', horribly ironic in retrospect?

Q What is the meaning of Lear's line, 'Let them anatomise Regan'?

Q What does the Fool's last line mean? (3.6.41)

3.7

Summary: *Gloucester is blinded.*

KEY SCENE

The 'blinding' scene is notorious for its graphic violence when Cornwall, following Gonerill's suggestion, tortures Gloucester for helping Lear. Gloucester finds out about Edmond's treachery and Edgar's innocence too late. A brave servant loses his life when he opposes the cruelty, but manages to mortally wound Cornwall.

Once blinded, Gloucester's capacity for 'seeing' with insight is activated. This makes possible his dramatically overwhelming 'Dover Cliff' scene with Edgar (see 4.5 below). This brutal act indicates how uncivilised and disordered the world has become, signalled initially by Lear's abdication of legitimate royal authority. Gloucester reminds Cornwall and Regan (and Shakespeare's original audience) several times that they are breaching the sacred rules of hospitality, known and respected from classical times, if they do him violence. There are obligations of trust to be honoured on both sides. Cornwall's acceptance of 'justice' stops just short of murder, but well short of a fair trial.

Q How could the blinding be staged today? Would a film version make the scene easier or harder to realise?

4.1

Summary: Edgar, still in disguise, comes to his father's aid.

KEY SCENE

'Tis the time's plague when madmen lead the blind (4.1.47).

Edgar, alone, expresses his feeling of being at the very lowest point in his life. Then he meets his blind father, who wants to be led to a cliff at Dover – and the loving son decides he must continue to play 'Poor Tom'.

Q How does Edgar cope with his despair?

Q Why can't Edgar reveal his true identity to Gloucester at this point?

4.2

Summary: Albany learns of Cornwall's death and of Gloucester's blinding.

Gonerill and Edmond, whom she desires, mock her husband Albany's failure to act like a soldier. A letter from Regan (now widowed) arrives, activating Gonerill's jealous response. Who will have the better claim to Edmond?

Q What is Albany's complex response to the news that Gloucester was blinded?

4.3

Summary: Cordelia returns with the desire to help Lear.

Queen Cordelia, leading a French army, has invaded Britain not to conquer but to rescue and heal Lear. She explains that she's fighting a war that his folly instigated, out of 'dear love' for him.

Q What new features of Cordelia's character are demonstrated in this scene?

4.4

Summary: Regan presses her claim to marry Edmond.

Regan gives a letter to Oswald to inform his mistress that *she* is fitter (as Cornwall's widow) to marry Edmond. She suggests Oswald might be rewarded if he finds the 'blind traitor' Gloucester.

Q What is Oswald's attitude to Regan in this scene? What can you infer from verbal cues?

4.5

Summary: *Gloucester arrives at Dover.*

KEY SCENE

The long 'Dover Cliff' scene evolves in several dramatic steps.

- As he leads his blind father, Edgar (still disguising his voice but no longer the madman 'Poor Tom') vividly describes the walk as though it is a steep and dangerous climb to the cliff top. Gloucester thinks he is throwing himself to his death and faints as he falls forward.
- When Gloucester revives, Edgar (taking on another voice) convinces him that he did in fact fall to the bottom of the cliff and that his 'life's a miracle'. Because he cannot verify this by sight, Gloucester accepts that he must 'bear affliction' patiently.
- Lear joins them: the two old men engage in a disturbingly cruel, sad dialogue of shared grief. Note the clusters of thematic imagery here.
- A Gentleman sent by Cordelia finds Lear, who runs away. Then, when Oswald (carrying Gonerill's letter to Edmond) appears and tries to seize Gloucester as a prize, Edgar (disguising his voice again as a peasant) fights and kills Oswald.

Q Notice how often Edgar addresses Gloucester as 'father' from this scene until the end. Halio notes that this is just a way of addressing an old man politely but do you think it could indicate more than that? Edgar cannot yet reveal himself but he has the comfort of at least addressing Gloucester as his own father.

Q Could the Gentleman's news that Cordelia's army has gone on ahead of her (while she searches for Lear) make the audience start to feel uneasy about the military outcome and prepare them for the play's ending?

4.6

Summary: *Lear and Cordelia are reunited.*

'Where have I been? Where am I? Fair daylight?' (4.6.49)
'If you have poison for me, I will drink it.' (4.6.70)

Lear is terrified and unable to grasp where he is. Kent and Cordelia work hard to restore Lear's sense of himself as a living man and a king. He asks them to 'Forget/ and forgive' (4.6.81–2).

5.1

Summary: *Albany and Edmond unite against Cordelia's army.*

KEY SCENE

As the sisters' armies gather, Regan extracts a brief promise of commitment from Edmond. Gonerill and Regan are vicious in open rivalry for him. Albany voices misgivings about fighting his king (5.1.16–18). Edmond's soliloquy sets out his dilemma ('Which of them shall I take?') and informs us that Albany, as the senior noble, is being manipulated to justify the war. Edmond's security depends on eliminating Albany.

Q Why is Albany dithering? How do Edgar's conversation with him and the letter (from Gonerill to Edmond, carried by Oswald) alter the situation?

Q How does Edgar's intervention with news of a mysterious 'champion' prepare the audience for a new strand of chivalric romance in the concluding scene?

5.2

Summary: *Cordelia's army is defeated.*

Men must endure/ Their going hence even as their coming hither;/ Ripeness is all (5.2.9–11)

The scene neatly depicts a conventional Elizabethan dramatic suggestion of a big battle in progress, with characters passing 'over the stage'. The battle's disastrous outcome, reported by Edgar, is that Lear and Cordelia have been captured. Edgar's impulse is to keep Gloucester strong-minded but accepting, and away from physical danger.

Q Edgar's last three lines, ending with 'Ripeness is all', are often quoted as indicative of one of the play's central messages about life. Gloucester's final response is usually edited out. Does his line 'And that's true too' add anything to our understanding of Gloucester's character or to the dramatic message?

5.3

Summary: *Lear dies of grief over the death of Cordelia.*

KEY SCENE

This scene evolves in six steps:

- As Edmond's prisoners, Cordelia and Lear are in grave danger, yet they console each other bravely: 'We are not the first/ Who with best meaning have incurred the worst' (Cordelia, 5.3.3–4). The audience's concerns are borne out by Edmond's advice to his captain to be 'as the time is' (5.3.32) and kill the prisoners.

  Q Contrast the tone of Lear's speeches with Cordelia's and Edmond's speeches with the Captain. How do the two sets of speakers see the world and value the experience of life?

- Albany sets off a quarrel between Regan and Gonerill when he snubs Edmond as a subordinate, then arrests him for treason. Regan would fight for him now if she felt stronger.

  Q Why does Regan make a point of telling us (three times) that she feels sick?

- Gonerill's sneering comment, 'An Interlude!' (5.3.83, see **Background** notes above), when Albany attempts to assert himself against Edmond, is a more accurate dramatic metaphor than she intends. It introduces the moral duel to restore right that Edgar has primed Albany to inaugurate. When the trumpet sounds, Albany throws down the gauntlet, signalling Edgar to appear *incognito* in armour and the episode commences. In summoning this unnamed knight as a champion against Edmond, Albany stage manages a tournament that will bring about the conclusion of the Gloucester plot.

  Q Notice the tonal shift in language, with Edgar's antiquated formulaic delivery of his challenge to Edmond, who accepts with similar formality. Why is the audience's attention being drawn to the ritualised nature of this *denouement*?

- When Edmond falls wounded, the scene's language reverts to contemporary argumentative patterning as the tragic events accumulate. Gonerill tries to defend herself against Albany's accusations (based on the incriminating letter given to him by Edgar). After she rushes offstage in defeated rage, Edmond hears Edgar's account of Gloucester's suffering and the circumstances of his death. A Gentleman brings in a 'bloody knife', by which Gonerill has committed suicide. He also brings news that Regan is dead.

Q What brings about a change in Edmond in this part of the scene?

- It is a theatrical masterstroke to delay Kent's entrance in Act 5 until a hundred lines before the play's end. Readers and audience alike have almost forgotten his character, as he hasn't appeared since 4.6, well before the battle. After the distraction of the sisters' deaths and Edmond's last boast (about their rivalry in love for him), Kent poses the obvious question – where's Lear? After a terrible moment of fumbling, Albany, Edgar and the dying Edmond dispatch an officer to the prison.

Q Why do you think Albany makes an appeal to the gods to 'defend' Cordelia at this moment?

- Lear carries Cordelia onstage in his arms, calling to mind (some critics argue) images reminiscent of a *pieta*. Is Cordelia dead? The audience would know that Shakespeare's sources let her survive this battle. Lear tries to ascertain whether she still lives, while the onlookers remain unsure about how deluded he is. Kent, especially, struggles to bear the painful disappointment of being reunited with an old master who cannot fully recognise his faithful servant Caius. Albany, Kent and Edgar are left to repair the 'gored state' as Lear dies, and find new purpose in their damaged lives.

Q What do you think Kent means when he asks 'Is this the promised end?' (5.3.237)

Q What has happened to the Fool? Consider the significance of Lear's statement: 'And my poor fool is hanged' (5.3.279). Is he referring to the Fool or Cordelia?

Q What kind of king do you think Edgar will be?

CHARACTERS & RELATIONSHIPS

King Lear

Key Quotes

I am a man/ More sinned against than sinning (3.2.57–8)

No, they cannot touch me for crying. I am the king himself (4.5.83)

I am even/ The natural fool of fortune (4.5.182–3)

Laurence Olivier, playing Lear for Granada TV when he was 80 and terminally ill, said, 'When you're younger, Lear doesn't feel real. When you get to my age you are Lear in every nerve of your body' (A Leggatt 1991, p.127). The play charts a massive psychological awakening for Lear, changing from petulant autocrat who thinks he's invincible to a vulnerable but stately man who comes to understand how deeply flawed and pitiful humanity can be. The play begins with Lear at the end of a long life: his foolish mistake in dividing a kingdom between his supposedly 'loving daughters' on the evidence of a spurious verbal declaration is inconsistent with the decision of a competent ruler.

His experiential journey takes him from being king to being a grieving, raging 'nothing' in a storm, then to a deranged but oddly perceptive 'sovereignty' when he meets Gloucester in 4.5. He is granted a last brief episode of peace with Cordelia just before death. Does he relapse into madness at the end – or just let go of life?

Lear and his daughters

Key Quotes

Yet he hath ever but slenderly known himself (Regan, 1.1.84–5)

The best and soundest of his time hath been but rash (Gonerill agrees, 1.1.286)

How honest are Regan and Gonerill about Lear's rashness? Is there something in what they say, that shouldn't be overlooked in his personality? Has he always had an erratic streak in him? How has this affected Gonerill and Regan? Cordelia caustically names her duplicitous sisters 'the jewels of our father' (1.1.262) but warns them, 'I know you, what you are' (1.1.263). What are they? And why is Cordelia different?

Gonerill

Key Quotes

By day and night, he wrongs me (1.3.4)

Oh, the difference of man and man (comparing Albany and Edmond, 4.2.27)

You are not worth the dust which the rude wind/ Blows in your face (Albany, 4.2.32)

Gonerill, the eldest and least-loved daughter, plays Lear's game suavely to get the reward he's offering – then turns icy after he's stripped of his power (1.4). She is guilty of ingratitude, although Lear's representation of himself as 'Your old kind father, whose frank heart gave all' (3.4.20) fails to acknowledge the explicit obligation contingent on the gift, which she sees only too clearly. Because his style of communication with her is to bully and threaten, she holds no love for him in return. Her fears about his private army of a hundred knights may be justified. She says she knows his heart.

Gonerill has no loving connection in the world, which makes Lear's terrible curse on her (of barrenness or an unloving child) exceptionally pointed (1.4.230–44). She despises her husband, Albany, because he is too soft – unlike the sexually attractive man of action, Edmond. Her polite coolness to Lear in 2.4 stems from having Regan as her ally. When Edmond, who first pledged himself to her, turns to Regan, the ally becomes a rival. Exposed as a treacherous wife and cornered in 5.3, she briefly tries to assert her authority as the rightful queen ('the laws are mine, not thine') before leaving the stage to kill herself.

Gonerill's mirror

Halio notes that at several points in the F text there's a suggestion that Gonerill is to be associated with the sin of female pride (vanity) and probably has the habit of using a small mirror, hanging from her belt, to check her appearance. Albany calls her a 'gilded serpent' (5.3.78) and Kent characterises her as 'Vanity the puppet' (2.2.32). The image of a woman looking into her mirror and seeing either a devil reflected back (instead of her own face) or peering over her shoulder and smiling at her reflection, was a common emblem of the sin of Pride or Vanity in mediaeval and Renaissance art.

Lear and Gonerill

Key quotes

She hath … struck me with her tongue/ Most serpent-like upon the very heart (Lear tells Regan, 2.4.152–3)

But yet thou art my flesh, my blood, my daughter,/ Or rather a disease that's in my flesh/ Which I must needs call mine (2.4.214–16)

Lear's relationship with Gonerill is disturbed from the beginning. He addresses her formally, without endearments, and makes no comment on her proclamations of love in 1.1. Gonerill is unfortunate to be the second child to oppose his wishes. With his fatherly pride already damaged by Cordelia's insubordination, Lear is now 'struck' by another 'serpent' he thought he'd mastered. He begins a litany of curses on his eldest 'degenerate bastard', calling down upon her barrenness, lameness, blindness and ugliness. She is referred to as a boil, a plague sore and a swollen tumour, something he unconsciously admits is in his 'corrupted blood'.

Gonerill's husband, Duke of Albany

KEY QUOTES

I must change names at home and give the distaff / Into my husband's hands (4.2.17–18)

My fool usurps my body (Gonerill's view of her husband, 4.2.29)

Great thing of us forgot! (5.3.210)

Albany has comparatively few lines in the play but is held in high authority. He reminds us, by his natural formality of speech, that he still considers Lear as 'the king' and is openly critical of 'the rigour of our state' (5.1.16–17) under the sisters' rule.

Gonerill despises the 'cowish terror of his spirit' (4.2.13) and his timidity. 'He'll not feel wrongs/ Which tie him to an answer' (4.2.14–15) is a neat formulation for someone who prefers to keep out of trouble, as Albany has done up to this point. Albany is careful about not showing his hand too soon – he never assumes that Cordelia's French forces and popular support for Lear will defeat the sisters. Edmond implies that he's prepared for Albany's move in his soliloquy (5.1.54–8). Does Albany think that his authority will be sufficient, whatever the outcome, to protect Lear and Cordelia? Their safety slips from his mind at the crucial moment (5.3.210).

When Gonerill suggests that Albany should hold her distaff, she is degrading her husband's virility. A distaff is a simple tool for winding wool, denoting women's domestic work, and often (because of its phallic shape) turned into an indecent joke. Shakespeare's audiences would pick up a common allusion to 'distaff Hercules' in her words. This was a well-known classical story of the great hero unmanned by slavish love for

Queen Omphale, who dressed him up in her gown and made him spin wool while she put on his armour and went off to fight.

The worm turns in 4.2, where Gonerill's aggressive plans against him and news of Gloucester's blinding finally activate Albany's resistance. He believes in divine justice and dedicates himself to be its instrument to help Lear and avenge Gloucester (4.2.63–5) – but in reality does very little apart from assisting Edgar and exposing Edmond's and Gonerill's plotting.

Regan

Key Quote

I am made of that self-mettle as my sister/ And prize me at her worth (1.1.64–5)

Although she seems softer than Gonerill, Regan's subtle cruelty is notable from the beginning in several ways. Her proclamation of love undermines Gonerill's, while laying claim to everything her sister has said, 'only she comes too short' (1.1.67). She recommends that Kent be kept in the stocks overnight, and makes a joke when he points out the severity of the punishment (2.2.23–125). She calmly reduces Lear's followers to none (2.4.256). Gloucester calls her 'unmerciful lady' at the beginning of his ordeal in 3.7: she taunts him by plucking his beard, then encourages Cornwall to destroy both eyes, again with a joke. She doesn't hesitate to kill the 'peasant' who dares to fight Cornwall and derives sadistic pleasure in informing Gloucester of Edmond's betrayal.

Regan is destroyed as much by her lust and jealousy as by Gonerill's poison, which takes effect during their squabble over Edmond in 5.3.

Lear and Regan

Key Quotes

No, Regan, thou shalt never have my curse (2.4.163)

I pray you, father, being weak, seem so (2.4.194)

Regan is Lear's last hope after disowning Cordelia and Gonerill. He addresses her fondly as 'Our dearest Regan' in 1.1, is reluctant to speak or think ill of her and never curses her individually (when he finally snaps, both she *and* Gonerill are 'unnatural hags'). He resorts to a wheedling tone to plead with her. Regan's ploy is to emphasise his age and weakness. Notice how Lear says to her (using the familiar form) '**thou** better know'st / The offices of nature, bond of childhood,/ Effects of courtesy, dues of gratitude' (than Gonerill) (2.4.170–2).

Regan's husband, Duke of Cornwall

Key Quotes

You know the fiery quality of the Duke (Gloucester to Lear, 2.4.85)

The revenges we are bound to take upon your father are not fit for your beholding (to Edmond, 3.7.7–8)

Cornwall is an arrogant, vicious thug and a fitting husband for Regan. The audience can only feel that justice has been done when he's mortally wounded by a servant as he's blinding Gloucester. Regan encourages Cornwall's violence.

He justifies maiming Gloucester by arguing that, while he's aware of the law, he just wants to vent his sadistic rage: 'We may not pass upon his life/ Without the form of justice, yet our power/ Shall do a curtsy to our wrath, which men/ May blame but not control' (3.7.24–7).

Cordelia

Key Quotes

What shall Cordelia speak? Love and be silent (1.1.57)

No blown ambition doth our arms incite,/ But love, dear love, and our aged father's right (4.3.27–8)

We are not the first/ Who with best meaning have incurred the worst (5.3.3–4)

Although she is the unintentional but crucial motivator in the main plot, Cordelia has a small speaking part and is offstage for most of the play. Her concern for Lear brings her back from France. She returns to the action in 4.3 as a Queen leading her own army and nurses Lear back to a fragile sanity. Shakespeare departs from his *Leir* sources when he has Cordelia killed on Edmond's orders. This would come as a shock to his original audience, who knew from Holinshed that Cordeilla [sic] became Queen after Leir's death and ruled for five years until challenged by her nephews. Then she was deposed and imprisoned. She hanged herself in despair. Shakespeare puts Cordelia forward as a model of virtue and transfers the suicidal despair to Gloucester.

Cordelia's dramatic strength in 1.1 is evident in her brave firmness and unwavering love for her father. Although she expresses a range of recognisable human feelings, her role takes on increasingly symbolic significance as Lear's saviour: 'O dear father,/ It is thy business that I go about' (4.3.23–4), suggesting analogies with Christ. Notice how her most significant lines are rhymed couplets, a break with the natural-sounding flow of blank verse.

Read the versified story of Cordila [sic] in *The Mirror for Magistrates* by John Higgins (1574), a collection of moral tales about 'the falles of the first infortunate Princes of this lande' (in Bullough, VII, pp.323–32). Interestingly, this version of the tale is told as a first-person account.

Lear and Cordelia

Key Quotes

Our joy, although our last and least (1.1.77–8)

O most small fault,/ How ugly didst thou in Cordelia show! (1.4.221–2)

I killed the slave that was a-hanging thee (5.3.248)

Lear wants Cordelia to please him – he knows she loves him, so the game is unnecessary. But she refuses to make hollow protestations: for that 'small fault' she is banished and Lear's mental collapse begins. We feel relief when she comes back in 4.3, speaking with calm authority (using the royal plural), knowing her father is 'mad as the vexed sea' and ready to help him. Her gentle love is apparent in 4.6, where she asks that her lips can 'kiss' medicine into him and 'repair the violent harms that my two sisters/ Have in thy reverence made' (4.6.26–9).

Act 5.3 is a devastating conclusion, even though Lear reports with a flash of grim glee that he killed Cordelia's murderer. Finally he recalls her voice, 'ever soft,/ Gentle, and low, an excellent thing in woman' (5.3.246–7).

Cordelia's husband, the King of France

KEY QUOTE

> Love's not love/ When it is mingled with regards that stands/ Aloof from
> th'entire point (1.1.233–5)

France appears only in the first scene of the play but his integrity is memorable. He creates a still centre of honest love for Cordelia, matching her own in a scene otherwise seething with smiling hypocrisy and violent emotions. He chooses to marry Cordelia 'this unprized precious maid' (1.1.254) because he loves her, and the 'cold'st neglect' (1.1.249) she suffers only makes his love 'kindle to inflamed respect' (1.1.250). Unlike Burgundy, who was obviously in it for the dowry, France understands that Cordelia's value as a wife is intrinsic – 'she is herself a dowry' (1.1.236).

France helps the audience realise how irrational Lear's punishment of Cordelia is, and tries to restore her to her father's favour by reminding Lear how he used to praise Cordelia as 'the best, the dearest ... balm of [his] age' (1.1.208–10). Later he makes good his vow that Cordelia will be made 'queen of us, of ours, and our fair France' (1.1.252) when he supports her action to return to England, leading his country's army, to rescue Lear.

Lear's Fool

KEY QUOTES

> Since my young lady's going into France, sir, the fool hath much pined away
> (Knight, 1.4.63)
>
> I would fain learn to lie (1.4.141)
>
> I am a fool, thou art nothing (to Lear, 1.4.153)

Every scene the Fool appears in is full of significant material; everything he says is important. His character is memorable despite having relatively few lines. He looms large in the imagination, well beyond the size of his dramatic role.

The Fool is obliged to be a truth-speaker, which he claims makes him unpopular and likely to get beaten for every utterance (1.4.143–4). Lear depends on him to understand what is happening and keep communicating the truth obliquely, to accompany him like a loving child into emotional turmoil. Lear articulates his emotional need for both the Fool and Cordelia in 1.4 and 5.3.

The Fool uses his mental ingenuity to find strangely appropriate analogies for cruel truths. For example, he sees how Gonerill and Regan are like cuckoos in the nest – they've supplanted Lear's 'true' daughter – and warns how darkness inevitably follows when the candle (light, reason, civilisation and human bonds) is snuffed out (1.4.177). In the storm, the Fool's utterances become surreal. His 'prophesy' speech (3.2.79–92) is filled with social commentary not unlike William Blake's. Read his lines carefully.

Pay attention to the Fool's last spoken line at 3.6.41 – what does he mean? Is it, as Halio's notes suggest, an 'inversion-statement', showing that the world is all topsy-turvy and he'll just do as Lear does? Nothing more is known, because Gloucester's urgent warning for Lear's safety has to be acted upon immediately. Does the Fool go along with the others or wander off alone? Is he caught and hanged? Or does he hang himself when he's abandoned (as the 2001 Shakespeare's Globe production suggested)?

Note: Read Halio's notes on Antony Sher's 'red-nosed clown' death in the 1982 RSC production (Introduction and photo, pp.48–9). Find **The Oval Cartoon Shakespeare** *King Lear* (1984), a graphic comic with full text. The illustrator Ian Pollock bases his disturbing character images on the RSC cast.

Fools were a feature of noble households in Shakespeare's time and James I brought his Scottish Fool with him to the English court. Read Enid Welsford, *The Fool. His social and Literary History* (1935, reprinted 1961).

The Earl of Kent ('Caius')

Key Quotes

Be Kent unmannerly/ When Lear is mad! (1.1.139–40)

You stubborn, ancient knave, you reverend braggart (Cornwall, 2.2.115)

He said it would be thus, poor banished man (Gloucester, 3.4.148)

Your servant Kent. Where is your servant Caius? (5.3.257)

Banished by Lear for defending Cordelia, Kent returns in disguise as 'Caius' (suggesting a stoical 'Roman' personality) to follow and protect his old master. He dares to confront Cornwall's sneering put-down of plain speaking (2.2.85–94) by parodying a flatterer (2.2.95–8), and then insults

Cornwall with the disparaging 'Ajax' comment (2.2.113), for which he is punished in the stocks. Instinctively sensing 'antipathy', he aggressively confronts Oswald twice in two days (1.4 and 2.2).

Kent takes punishment philosophically because he has known hardship and can tolerate worse than this overnight humiliation. He uses his time in the stocks as an opportunity to read Cordelia's letter and hopes Fortune will 'turn [her] wheel' soon (2.2.156). His unwavering love for Lear is crucial to the dramatic force of the last moments of Act 5. He notices Lear's absence and interrupts Albany's fussing over the sisters' dead bodies with an urgent enquiry. Albany suddenly remembers the 'great thing of us forgot!' (5.3.208–10).

We notice gentle dramatic irony when Gloucester tells Caius how 'that good Kent' prophesised the outcome of Lear's folly. Later, in another ironic moment, Lear greets Kent but – as much as Kent aches to explain – doesn't connect him with Caius, the faithful servant who he believes is 'dead and rotten' (5.3.259). Kent, an honest man who habitually expresses strong emotions, barely controls his agitation: 'All's cheerless, dark and deadly' (5.3.264). He understands Lear's desire for release from life because he shares it, having followed Lear's 'sad steps' from the 'first of difference and decay' to the 'rack of this tough world' (5.3.288–9).

The Duke of Burgundy

Key Quotes

Love's not love/ When it is mingled with regards that stands/ Aloof from th'entire point (1.1.233–5)

Burgundy, who appears only in 1.1, is a proud materialistic nobleman who rejects Cordelia as a potential wife when Lear disowns her, leaving her with no dowry. Cordelia cuts through his polite formulation of an excuse, aware that 'respect and fortune are his love' (1.1.243).

The Earl of Gloucester

Key Quotes

Love cools, friendships fall off, brothers divide (1.2.94, entire speech)

These injuries the king now bears will be revenged home (3.3.10)

I am tied to th'stake and I must stand the course (3.7.53)

Shakespeare develops the tragic relationship between Gloucester and his sons as a parallel sub-plot to Lear's family catastrophe. In contrast to Lear, whose suffering is predominantly mental, Gloucester undergoes severe physical violence. His description of himself 'tied to th'stake' evokes the cruelty of a bear-baiting pit (one was situated next to the Globe theatre), with himself as a doomed animal. Like Lear with Cordelia, the child Gloucester rejects (Edgar) is the one who truly loves him and helps him to greater acceptance of what life brings.

After witnessing Lear's mishandling of his heirs in 1.1, Gloucester becomes obsessed with portents of universal doom (1.2). His complaisant attitude to his own adult children is also primed to change. Edmond only has to feed his ageing father's negative fantasies about parricide (killing a father) to incriminate the legitimate heir. Once Edgar has been effectively alienated, Gloucester makes Edmond 'legitimate' by default, as the son who appears most loyal and dutiful.

Until he loses his eyes, Gloucester trusts Edmond and is metaphorically blind to the reality around him. He remains loyal to the old king, recognising the 'unnatural' malice of Cornwall, Regan and Gonerill, but still confides in Edmond about Cordelia's return. Paradoxically, the blinded Gloucester begins to truly 'see' when he falls into despair as Regan informs him of Edmond's betrayal: 'O, my follies!' (3.7.90).

Gloucester's attempted suicide at Dover Cliff (4.5) is his great turning point from despair to acceptance – but it's a rough transition for him and for Edgar, who still conceals his identity. Gloucester can't ever know that Edgar tricked him to thwart his suicide attempt.

During the battle, Gloucester blesses Edgar – 'Grace go with you, sir' (5.2.4) – before he is left alone onstage. The audience contemplates Gloucester's terrifying vulnerability. After a pause he is swept up and hurried away by Edgar, who informs him that the battle is lost. After a momentary temptation to succumb to 'ill thoughts', Gloucester rallies enough to endure at Edgar's prompting. He completes Edgar's half line 'Ripeness is all. Come on' with the philosophical response, 'And that's true, too' (5.2.11). Edgar later recounts how Gloucester died 'twixt two extremes of passion, joy and grief'. It seems that he has achieved the 'ripeness' Edgar named, that mixed sense of peace (finally recognising his son) and acceptance of death.

Edmond

Be Kent unmannerly/ When Lear is mad! (1.1.139–40)

You stubborn, ancient knave, you reverend braggart (Cornwall, 2.2.115)

He said it would be thus, poor banished man (Gloucester, 3.4.148)

Your servant Kent. Where is your servant Caius? (5.3.257)

Edmond's character recalls the Vice figure from Morality plays and Interludes, whose dramatic purpose was to entice gullible souls (including the audience), and collect damned souls for hell. Shakespeare gives Edmond an outwardly personable and sexually attractive wickedness but adds further dimensions to the villain through revealing soliloquies and his startling deathbed discovery of a conscience.

Edmond is a selfish young pragmatist – he does what has to be done to get what he wants. He betrays his father to Cornwall without hesitation (though with a hypocritical show of anguish) because he believes that 'the younger rises when the old doth fall' (3.3.22).

His quick intelligence serves a single purpose – to oust his half-brother, 'legitimate Edgar' from Gloucester's affections and take his inheritance by any means, including betrayal. He despises his 'credulous father' and Edgar's 'foolish honesty' because they are so easy to manipulate. For example, he plays easily on Gloucester's superstitious fears by conjuring up a chilling image of Edgar, sword out, praying to the moon (2.1.38–9).

How much is Edmond affected by his illegitimacy? The audience must feel uncomfortable for his sake in 1.1, when Gloucester talks to Kent about the 'sport' that led to his conception.

By Act 5, Edmond's strategy to win the throne as well as his father's earldom depends on ensuring Gloucester is dead and both Lear and Cordelia are in his, not Albany's, control.

Edmond, Gonerill and Regan

Yours in the ranks of death (Edmond to Gonerill, 4.2.26)

I shall never endure her, Dear my lord,/ Be not familiar with her (Regan to Edmond. He replies: Fear me not (5.1.12–13)

> To both these sisters have I sworn my love ... Neither can be enjoyed/ If both remain alive (5.1.44–8)
>
> I was contracted to them both; all three/ Now marry in an instant (5.3.202–3)

Gonerill's jealousy of her sister Regan (now a widow) as an eligible rival for Edmond's affections is made apparent at end of 4.2. Regan is equally jealous of Gonerill, sending letters to Edmond via Oswald (4.4). Just before the battle (5.1) Regan warns Edmond to be faithful to her and leave the married Gonerill alone. She doesn't know that Albany is in possession of the letter Oswald was carrying to Edmond, which Edgar reads aloud to the audience (4.5.250–5).

The issue flares up openly in 5.3, ostensibly because Albany and Edmond tussle over who is in charge of Lear and Cordelia as prisoners. Albany refuses to acknowledge Edmond's authority to make any decisions because he's 'a subject' not 'a brother' (5.3.54–5). Regan weighs in to defend Edmond as her General, which incites Gonerill to challenge her, then Albany raises the issue of Edmond as a husband for Regan. On cue, Edgar arrives to challenge Edmond, Regan retires sick and Gonerill, exposed to shame, soon leaves to kill herself. While all this is going on, everyone (including the audience) is sidetracked into forgetting about Lear and Cordelia.

Edgar

Key Quotes

> Some villain hath done me wrong (1.2.138)
>
> Edgar I nothing am (2.3.21)
>
> Ripeness is all (5.3.11)

Key Point

When Gloucester asks 'Poor Tom', 'What are you?', the disguised Edgar replies that he is 'A most poor man, made tame to fortune's blows,/ Who by the art of known and feeling sorrows/ Am pregnant to good pity' (4.5.212–14). Edgar is genuinely capable of helping Gloucester accept 'fortune's blows' because he, too, has endured unjust suffering and become 'nothing'.

Edgar, Gloucester's legitimate son and heir, is led to believe (by Edmond's misinformation) that some villain has put him under suspicion as a traitor. Edmond is able to make his naive brother panic and flee from home. Edgar chooses the role of a mad beggar as his life-saving disguise (2.3).

'Poor Tom' describes his life history in a difficult key speech (3.4.77–90). Notice the human types 'Tom' characterises – sexual, predatory, materialistic, sinful. His world is ugly and dangerous. As the play develops, Edgar struggles to maintain the illusion of being 'Tom': 'I cannot daub it further … And yet I must' (4.1.52, 54). His capacity to maintain his persona's 'voice' diminishes under emotional stress: Gloucester notices 'Tom's' shift from gabbling prose to blank verse immediately – 'Methinks thy voice is altered, and thou speakst/ In better phrase and matter than thou didst' (4.5.7–8).

If we wonder why Edgar doesn't reveal his true identity at several opportunities, we need to think about how critical his disguise is in helping Gloucester psychologically and spiritually. Carefully re-read the Dover Cliff scene (4.5), where Edgar's word-pictures convince the blind Gloucester and the audience to see the location in the mind's eye. He then leads Gloucester out of his suicidal despair into acceptance. Do we feel hopeful when Edgar becomes Britain's new king?

Oswald

Key Quotes

You whoreson cullionly barber-monger (Kent, 2.2.29, 31)

[A] slave whose easy-borrowed pride/ Dwells in the sickly grace of her he follows (Lear's view, 2.4.178–9)

I know thee well – a serviceable villain,/ As duteous to the vices of thy mistress/ As badness would desire (Edgar, killing Oswald in defence of Gloucester, 4.5.240–2)

Characterised as an ambitious fop, Oswald appears in several scenes as Gonerill's Steward and letter-bearer. Kent immediately despises him as a coward, setting up a negative bias in the audience's mind. Kent describes Oswald as a courtly time-server (2.2.63–75), unwilling to get into a fight but 'brave' enough to insult Kent as an 'ancient ruffian' when other people are present.

Oswald tells Regan that Albany is reluctant to take an army against Cordelia and that Gonerill 'is the better soldier' (4.4.5). He won't give away too much of Gonerill's secret communication with Edmond, although Regan makes it clear it would be in Oswald's interest to dissuade Gonerill from pursuing Edmond. Oswald understands. He agrees that if he finds Gloucester ('that blind traitor'), he will kill him and so prove his loyalty to Regan.

At the end of 4.5 Edgar fights Oswald to save Gloucester from being taken prisoner. Before dying, Oswald instructs Edgar to deliver his incriminating letter from Gonerill to Edmond. This crucial document confirms Albany as a supporter of Lear and allows Edgar to set up the conditions for a challenge to Edmond in 5.3.

Curan

One of Gloucester's servants, he passes 'ear-kissing arguments' (rumours) to Edmond that Albany and Cornwall are likely to make war on each other (2.1.6–11). This war doesn't happen because they are forced into alliance against the invading French army (Kent has a letter from Cordelia about this by 2.2 and Gloucester has another by 3.3).

Cornwall's servant

Key Quotes

I have served you since I was a child/ But better service have I never done you/ Than now to bid you hold (3.7.72–4)

A peasant stand up thus! (Regan, 3.7.79)

This minor character is 'an ordinary hero', the anonymous brave moral voice raised in a horrifying scene. He's powerless to prevent Cornwall from blinding Gloucester: the important point is that he challenges Cornwall to 'take the chance of anger' (3.7.78) and, although he loses his life when Regan stabs him from behind, he is able to deal Cornwall a mortal blow.

Old Man

> Thy comforts can do me no good at all;/ Thee they may hurt (Gloucester, 4.1.16–17)
>
> You cannot see your way (4.1.17)

A minor anonymous character, the Old Man demonstrates the unbroken loyalty of a tenant to his lord, despite personal dangers (to which Gloucester alludes). He leads the blinded Gloucester towards Dover, until Edgar (as 'Poor Tom') takes over. His anxiety about blindness provokes Gloucester to express rueful but perceptive statements about sight.

Messenger

Arrives in 4.2. to bring important news to Albany about Cornwall's death and Gloucester's blinding. He also carries a letter from Regan to Gonerill.

THEMES, IDEAS & VALUES

Relationships

The main Lear plot and Gloucester sub-plot evolve along lines of relationship. Holding the two family groups together is the overarching idea of rule, the question of who controls the national 'family' in which individual families play out their own domestic dramas. The state of the metaphorical body-politic, with the ruler as its 'crowned head' governing all the individual parts, was a powerful image in Shakespeare's time.

The ideal ruler in Shakespeare is characterised as capable and just. Imagery about the human body illustrates the idea: if the head becomes corrupt, the body will sicken and fail, natural feelings and duties will break down into feral anarchy (as in *Hamlet* and *Macbeth*). A web of ideas about the interrelated structure of society, moral and ethical choices, individual beliefs and unseen influences, and about human relations with the natural world, all shape *King Lear*.

Ruler and subjects (the Divine Right of Kings)

Key Quote

They told me I was everything; 'tis a lie, I am not ague-proof (Lear, 4.5.101)

Bonds, responsibilities and obligations shape social relationships and make political reality. The ways in which they are honoured or neglected underpins the whole play.

James I's view on the relationship between the Ruler and God in a Christian society was that kingship was a solemn duty conferred by God's will on the recipient. Along with the responsibility for subjects came also the *Divine Right* to rule, creating unassailable authority. Although James' formulation of his powers was met with hostility and much discussion, it was in line with traditionally accepted ideas in England about royal authority in a Christian monarchy.

James I had the political sense to see that a union of his two kingdoms would strengthen his authority. Lear takes the reverse decision for politically naive, selfish reasons, principally his wish to be 'unburdened' (1.1.36). Such poor judgment is disastrous for a ruler who wants personal power without retaining the authority to ensure it.

The play presents a traditional view in Kent's response to the great mistake Lear has made. As far as he is concerned, Lear is still king and needs protecting from his act of temporary madness. When Kent reintroduces himself to Lear in disguise (1.4), he offers his service specifically because there is something intrinsic to Lear's 'countenance' that he 'would fain call master'. When Lear enquires what that is, Kent replies 'Authority' (1.4.17–27). Kent honours Lear threefold as king, father and master (1.1.134–5).

Parent and child

Key Quote

I love your majesty/ According to my bond (Cordelia, 1.1.87)

Family members, now as then, are united *and* divided by perceived duties observed or shunned, bonds honoured or broken, and feelings expressed, masked or withheld. In the play, Lear and Gloucester have such naive ideas about their adult children that a single event in each case precipitates a fatal crisis for the family group.

Cordelia's simple statement is unambiguous in its profound honesty but, because it avoids rhetoric and comes after a string of 'nothings', it is too bald an expression of love and filial obligation for Lear to absorb. Some critics argue that she is coldly correct and could have tried to explain herself better, missing the point that all the force of her message is in the word 'bond', which she takes seriously as a sacred unbreakable thing.

Child and parent

Key quotes

Our flesh and blood, my lord, is grown so vile/ That it doth hate what gets [begets] it (Gloucester to Lear, 3.4.129–30)

I know you do not love me (Lear to Cordelia, 4.6.71)

The two disgraced and rejected children in this play prove themselves to be the most loyal to their misguided fathers when other siblings turn violent. Edgar proves his love to Gloucester by forcing his father to confront and overcome despair at Dover Cliff (4.5). Cordelia returns from France as a warrior queen: Lear expects her to hate him, with just cause, but instead she offers forgiveness (4.6).

Gloucester's observation to Lear about their children hating them is made in Edgar's hearing – his 'Poor Tom' outburst is the only way he can communicate his anguished protest yet remain unrecognised.

When the blinded Gloucester calls out for Edmond to 'enkindle the sparks of nature/ To quit this horrid act' (3.7.85–6), Regan has the sadistic pleasure of inflicting pain on yet another father, by revealing Edmond's duplicity. In anguish, Gloucester finally understands: 'O, my follies! Then Edgar was abused' (3.7.90–1).

Key quotes

As much as child e'er love or father found (Gonerill, 1.1.54)

I find she names my very deed of love (Regan 1.1.66)

Look carefully at the hypocritical excesses of Gonerill's and Regan's artful public speeches. How precisely does each one estimate her quantity of love? What they say is grotesquely absurd. If Lear were not deaf to criticism, he might detect the insincerity. It is left to Cordelia to observe and try to heal the 'untuned and jarring senses' of her 'child-changèd father' (4.6.17).

Siblings

> I know you what you are/ And like a sister am most loath to call/ Your faults as they are named (Cordelia, 1.1.263)
>
> He always loved our sister most (Gonerill to Regan, 1.1.281)
>
> Brother, I advise you for the best. I am no honest man, if there be any good meaning towards you. (Edmond to Edgar, 1.2.145)
>
> I am no less in blood than thou art, Edmond./ If more, the more th'hast wronged me. (Edgar, after their duel, 5.3.157–8)

Gonerill and Regan are impolite to Cordelia and resentful of her position as the favourite child. Edmond appears to support Edgar like a brother, even wounding himself to add verisimilitude to their supposed fight. The bastard son wants what an accident of birth denies him. Edgar challenges Edmond with being 'false to the gods, thy brother, and thy father'.

Social bonds

> We have seen the best of our time. Machinations, hollowness, treachery, and all ruinous disorders follow us disquietly to our graves (Gloucester, 1.2.99–100)

Society is only as stable as its individual members, how intelligently they understand their world and how willing they are to trust each other and work together. This is as true now as in Shakespeare's time. Lear's act of renunciation has destabilised relationships but, according to Gloucester, it is only one manifestation of a deeper malaise in the kingdom.

Gonerill, Regan and Cornwall are sociopaths. They have no qualms about ignoring the deepest moral obligations of social living, honoured from classical times. They injure their host (Gloucester is blinded in his own house), deny hospitality in need (they turn Gloucester, Lear, Kent and the Fool out into the stormy night) and renounce duties of loyalty and kinship.

Regan makes a great show of being polite to Gloucester as 'our good old friend' (2.1.125) but later plucks his beard, an act of utter disrespect. He is genuinely hospitable to them, though increasingly anxious for Lear, whom he still calls 'the king' (2.4.289). Regan suggests to him that his own house isn't big enough to shelter Lear as the storm begins (2.4). Gonerill agrees that Lear's wilfulness has led to his being shut out. Finally, Cornwall orders Gloucester, against his will, to shut his doors.

Nature

Shakespeare uses the word 'nature' in a number of ways, as we still do. The working of the natural world, its plants, living creatures, geographical environments and weather conditions, is one thematic strand in the play's imagery. Another theme builds on the reality that all living things are subject to a natural cycle, which brings things into being and ends them – whether from seeds to the finished crop ploughed back into the soil or from human birth to death. Shakespeare also makes his characters speculate on human nature, and how the reasoning mind (which supposedly separates people from beasts and establishes humanity) continually struggles to control and understand the clamour of feelings, drives and needs that we share with all other living creatures.

The human animal

Key Quote

Is man no more than this? ... thou art the thing itself
(Lear about naked 'Tom', 3.4.92–5)

To a deranged but still perceptive Lear, a mad naked beggar is more than a symbol of humanity brought low – he is 'the thing itself'. Tom ought to be better off dead (at least he'd be sheltered in a grave), yet he still clings to life. Lear feels he has something to learn from this 'philosopher'.

Key Quote

Let me wipe it first; it smells of mortality (4.5.129)

As blind Gloucester struggles forward with joy to kiss his master's hand, Lear holds him back and makes a telling comment on what he's learnt through madness about the reality of being human, with a body destined to age and die. Even a king's hand is subject to natural decay. Look for frequent references to mortality.

O ruined piece of nature! This great world shall so wear out to naught
(4.5.130–1)

Gloucester imagines that through Lear's disintegration he sees what everything in the natural world must come to in the end.

Human nature

I will forget my nature. So kind a father! (Lear, 1.5.2)

Natures of such deep trust we shall much need (Cornwall, about Edmond's loyalty, 2.1.115)

Both Lear and Cornwall refer to nature as intrinsic personality. Lear confuses a 'kind' parental nature with egocentric manipulation of his daughters. Edmond has no loyalty to Cornwall, other than that which will gain him the reward of his father's title. Lear in madness speculates whether 'anatomising Regan' (cutting her body open to examine the physical organs) would reveal the answer to her hard-hearted nature (3.6.34).

'Natural' feelings and needs

Allow not nature more than nature needs/ Man's life is cheap as beast's
(2.4.259–60)

Gonerill and Regan cruelly reduce Lear's entourage from one hundred knights to none, provoking his key speech, 'Oh, reason not the need'. What do humans truly need? What is it in our nature to crave? Lear begins to realise that he desperately requires patience to comprehend unpleasant truths about life and himself (2.4.264).

Kent and Cordelia both use an image of ill-treated dogs to define human callousness. Kent in the stocks accuses Regan: 'Why, madam, if I were your father's dog,/ You should not use me so' (2.2.124–5) and Cordelia defines the lack of kindness shown to Lear on the night of the storm, 'Mine enemy's dog,/ Though he had bit me, should have stood that night/ Against my fire' (4.6.33–5).

KEY QUOTE

I tax you not, you elements, with unkindness (3.2.15)

Kindness as a word suggests 'being part of humankind' as well as behaving kindly. Hence, Lear is unhurt by the storm's buffeting because it doesn't owe him any kindness or gratitude. Instead, he accuses his 'pelican daughters' of ripping their parent's breast (3.4.70), inverting an image from the mediaeval bestiary which connects the way pelican chicks were thought to feed from the parent bird and, by analogy, Christ feeds his 'children' with his blood.

KEY QUOTE

Our foster-nurse of nature is repose,/ The which he lacks (4.3.12–13)

The Gentleman with Cordelia understands that nature can heal itself if Lear's 'bereavèd sense' (4.3.9) is allowed something else it needs – rest. She suggests medicinal herbs '[a]ll you unpublished virtues of the earth' to help – and offers her tears to water the earth like Mother Nature, to help them grow (4.3.16–17).

Natural or legitimate?

KEY QUOTE

Loyal and natural boy (Gloucester, 2.1.83)

Social attitudes to illegitimacy depend on moral and ethical ideas prevalent at the time. A 'natural child' is a term for a child born out of wedlock. Negative connotations are carried by the term 'bastard', although the title of Royal Bastard was an honourable acknowledgment of a monarch's illegitimate child, who was well provided for but debarred from inheritance.

Edmond cynically plays on Gloucester's terror of parricide when he invents his description of Edgar's supposedly violent plan to inherit (1.2.45–52). He skilfully forestalls anything Edgar might challenge or deny by convincing Gloucester that Edgar will cite Edmond's 'unpossessing' bastard status to discredit his word against the legitimate heir's story. Gloucester believes Edmond, who is actually disloyal and 'unnatural' in his hatred of a father who loves him and has provided for him. Lear relegates all his disobedient legitimate daughters to the status of illegitimacy, calling Gonerill a 'degenerate bastard' (1.4.209).

Nature as goddess

Lear invokes the traditional Mother goddess in a shockingly inappropriate way, to curse Gonerill either with infertility or a malevolent child (1.4.230). Edmond, who has no belief in gods, wryly elevates his own will, the very force of Nature within him, to the equivalent status of goddess. He argues that he was conceived because it is in Nature's very nature to be 'lusty' and propagate. Compare Lear's similar thoughts in the storm, which lead back to Edmond: 'The wren goes to't ... let copulation thrive' (4.5.8–10).

The elemental storm

Key Quotes

One minded like the weather, most unquietly (Gentleman, 3.1.2)

The tyranny of the open night's too rough/ For nature to endure (Kent to Lear, 3.4.2–3)

Here's a night pities neither wise men nor fools (Fool, 3.2.12)

This tempest in my mind/ Doth from my senses take all feeling else,/ Save what beats there: filial ingratitude (Lear, 3.4.12–14)

Nature breaks in – and breaks down – in the fierce storm that gathers at the end of Act 2 and rages through Act 3. Note many lines that link the physical storm to Lear's breakdown. Kent observes that 'Man's nature cannot carry/ Th'affliction nor the fear (3.2.46–7) that such a violent event generates.

Lear in his full-blown madness engages completely with the elements to 'crack nature's moulds' and put an end to 'ingrateful man' (3.2.89). In 3.4 Lear challenges Kent's well-meaning concern about the need for physical shelter by making clear to us that his interior storm is much worse than the natural elements.

While Lear, the Fool, Tom and Kent battle with themselves, each other and the weather on the heath, the storm comes to Gloucester as he's blinded (3.7) and forced to experience his own 'tempest in the mind' – somewhere his eyes might never have taken him.

Age and wisdom

People accept ageing differently. Old age inevitably raises questions that have no easy answers and provokes thoughts about the purpose of an individual's life, what we've learnt, and how life will end. In traditional societies, age is associated with wisdom, something modern Western culture has lost. Is there a correlation? The play demonstrates that the journey to wisdom is a rough one but may be achieved in old age, if the mind and body can endure.

When the two broken old men meet again in 4.5, Lear struggles to offer comfort to Gloucester in an oblique way: 'If thou wilt weep my fortunes, take my eyes/ I know thee well enough; thy name is Gloucester./ Thou must be patient. We came crying hither ...' (4.5.168–70). How much do they deserve our pity for their follies?

Lear gives up being king because he says he wants to 'unburdened crawl towards death' (1.1.34–6). How near to death is this octogenarian? Both daughters reinforce his senile incompetence verbally, yet Gonerill seems genuinely concerned about Lear keeping his hundred knights to 'enguard his dotage with their powers/ And hold our lives in mercy' (1.4.280–1). When Lear playacts how he might beg Gonerill on his knees to forgive him for being old (2.4.146–8), his sarcasm is understood by Regan.

As usual, the Fool puts the brutal truth to Lear in 1.5: 'I'd have thee beaten for being old before thy time' (1.5.33) and, when Lear fails to pick it up, 'Thou shouldst not have been old till thou hadst been wise' (1.5.36). Lear should have known better (having lived long enough to become wise) than to give up his crown and expect to retain 'the name and all th'addition to a king' (1.1.130).

Edmond plays on Gloucester's insecurities about being old in his fake 'letter' from Edgar, which mentions the 'oppression of aged tyranny' (1.2.48). In contrast, Kent gets mocked as an 'old ruffian': in disguise he might look older than 44, but he is wise and far from senile.

Love

Can love be measured?

Lear's question to his daughters in 1.1 presupposes that he is somehow able to weigh each daughter's 'nature' (natural affection) against 'merit' (what she deserves). Despite being taken momentarily off guard, perhaps, Gonerill snaps into a rhetorically overblown but effective speech that serves the purpose. Regan follows suit. Cordelia cannot respond with a speech, although she understands the image of weighing implicit in the love test – it's just that her love is '[m]ore ponderous than [her] tongue' (1.1.72–3).

Must love be spoken?

Kent, Edgar and Cordelia demonstrate their love through action rather than words.

Cordelia's 'Love and be silent' (1.1.57) is the statement that precipitates Lear's mad assumption that she has 'nothing' to weigh. In contrast to the daughters' 'glib and oily' speeches, Kent's rude outburst paradoxically expresses the intensity of genuine love in words.

Notice other clusters of ideas about love associated with gratitude or ingratitude, respect or contempt, care or neglect. For example, the storm raises Lear's consciousness beyond his own sorrows to realise how 'poor naked wretches' suffer and how 'storms' (a divine agency) raise the consciousness of the rich of the world to be charitable: 'O I have ta'en/ Too little care of this' (3.4.32–3).

Sexuality and lust

Lust without love fires the sisters' rivalry over Edmond and marks his apparent unconcern about which one to choose. Edgar ties Gloucester's 'pleasant vices' in fathering Edmond to the working out of divine justice. Gloucester enjoyed his adultery but, as Edmond agrees, '[t]he dark and vicious place where thee he got/ Cost him his eyes' (5.3.60–3). The opposite experience is also part of reality: sexuality is reduced to 'copulation' without love in Lear's mind, reflecting his sorrow that legitimacy is no guarantee of genuinely caring offspring (4.5.110).

Gods and humans

The play is full of allusions to pagan gods yet the *Lear* universe has a strong Christian underpinning of sin, forgiveness and the virtue of suffering for the soul's growth. Almost every character has some comment on the gods, but which ones listen and where are they? You'll find much argument on the subject and no definitive answers.

Although there is some hope, such as Gloucester's 'good' death and Edgar's restoration, the play seems to happen in a cosmos without meaning or purpose. Humans alone are responsible for their own arbitrary acts of goodness or wickedness. Shakespeare denied his original audience the happy ending they expected – his plot ends distressingly for everyone left alive. What 'gods' will 'throw incense' [honour] on Cordelia's sacrifice?

Is human life dependent on divine will?

Although Gloucester speaks of divine will as 'great and opposeless' (4.5.38), his experience is so horrific that he fluctuates between bitter despair, 'As flies to wanton boys are we to th'gods;/ They kill us for their sport' (4.1.36–7), to prayer 'You ever gentle gods, take my breath from me./ Let not my worser spirit tempt me again/ To die before you please' (4.5.208–10). Edgar's guiding kindness helps his father to find equilibrium. The key scene is Dover Cliff (4.5).

Are the gods kind? Do they ever show mercy or pity? Cordelia and Gloucester may believe so: she prays to the 'kind gods' to cure Lear's 'abusèd nature' (4.6.14–15). When Gloucester discovers that Edgar is a good son, he prays, 'Kind gods, forgive me that, and prosper him' (3.7.91).

Several references to the gods have to be read ironically because they precede the complete reversal of a speaker's wishes. Lear appeals to old gods who will have sympathy with old men (2.4.182–5). He's proved wrong immediately when Regan and Gonerill unite against him. A most shocking irony follows Kent's thanks to Gloucester at the end of 3.6, 'The gods reward your kindness!' Gloucester is blinded in 3.7.

Are the gods interested in justice or judgment?

Somehow we know that Edmond's smirking hypocrisy in passing off his own treacherous views as Edgar's to Gloucester, 'I told him the revenging gods/ 'Gainst parricides did all the thunder bend' (2.1.44–5), will be believed. Acknowledging no gods, he has no fear of blasphemy.

Albany does believe in 'the judgement of the heavens, that makes us tremble', as he views his treacherous wife's body without pity (5.3.205–6). Moments later we see his desperate but apparently futile invocation to the gods to defend Cordelia.

Fortune

Like Mother Nature, Fortune with her turning wheel was one of the old mediaeval personifications, a goddess in classical times and still present in popular thought in Shakespeare's time. A popular image portrayed the Wheel of Fortune surrounded by crowned human figures. Sitting on top of the wheel is a king with the caption 'I rule', and sliding down the side is another (with his crown fallen off) – 'I have ruled'. Another king is crushed underneath the wheel at the bottom: 'I am without a kingdom'. Another figure reaching up on the ascending side says 'I shall rule'. Kent, the Fool, Edmond, Cordelia and Edgar all refer to fortune as a cyclic entity in life, which must be endured with patience. Lear imagines himself bound upon a 'wheel of fire' (4.6.44), changing Fortune's image to a strange instrument of torture.

Key Quote

For thee, oppressèd king, I am cast down,/ Myself could else outface false fortune's frown (Cordelia, 5.3.5–6)

Cordelia's speech pattern changes when she enters the classically heightened tragic finale. She knows that their fortune is in decline. By contrast, Lear's tone has become playfully free in its fantasy of prison life, ascending to the height of good fortune in achieving what he was aiming for in 1.1 – no burdens, just simple pleasure with Cordelia beside him. He still thinks they have a charmed immortality by their bond of love (5.3.8–25).

When Edmond confesses his and Gonerill's orders to have Cordelia hanged in prison and to 'lay the blame upon her own despair' (5.3.228), we know this is inconsistent with Shakespeare's Cordelia. She understands, like Edgar, that humans must be patient in the face of fortune's changes.

Nothing

Key Quote

Can you make no use of nothing, nuncle? (1.4.115)

Shakespeare manipulates the subtle nuances of the word 'nothing' throughout the play. This theme is concerned with how humans find and give value to life – and also how characters conceal 'something' as 'nothing'. In material terms or status, we may *have* nothing but does this mean we *are* 'nothing'? We are living creatures and so, paradoxically, always 'something'. The play is concerned with exploring these ideas. The Fool specifically targets Lear's narrow equation of having 'something' with material possessions. Lear goes mad because he thinks he has nothing if his daughters won't support him when they inherit 'his' kingdom. He can't bear to hear what Cordelia tells him about true value, nor when the Fool sets him straight. If Lear's measure of value is so superficial, then he truly has nothing and *is* nothing: 'Thou art an O without a figure ... I am a fool, thou art nothing' (1.4.152–3).

In the storm, Lear articulates some understanding that saying 'nothing' may actually be a mark of patience and the only appropriate response to a situation beyond a person's control (3.2.35–6). Learning to make something out of apparently nothing is a new experience for Lear: 'The art of our necessities is strange,/ And can make vile things precious' (3.2.68–9). Even an old hovel with other madmen is a good shelter for a king in a storm.

Compare Edmond's duplicitous use of the term as he echoes Cordelia's words in a different tone when he answers Gloucester's question with 'Nothing'. It is sufficient to alert the anxious Gloucester to an inferred 'something' (1.2.31).

Madness

Key Quote

O matter and impertinency mixed,/ Reason in madness (Edgar, observing Gloucester and Lear meet, 4.5.166–7)

Shakespeare's audience knew of mental disturbances such as melancholy, dementia, possession and hysteria (called 'the mother'). Lear names his sickness as he feels it coming on: 'O how this mother swells up toward my heart!' (2.4.52–3). Emotional shocks such as fear, grief or sudden awareness of one's own monumental folly destabilise Lear and Gloucester.

Edgar's shock at being hunted as a traitor must contribute to his choice of disguise, a man supposedly possessed by demons.

The professional Fool is also touched with insightful madness which he is able to express coherently: he can share conversations with deranged minds and find sense there (just as Edgar recognises 'reason in madness'). The Fool knows the difference between madness and folly. He perceives that anyone is vulnerable to emotional breakdown, given the right circumstances: a 'cold night will turn us all to fools and madmen' (3.4.72). Even he breaks down in silence by 3.6 and disappears, perhaps defeated by Lear's overwhelming madness.

Key Quote

We are not ourselves / When nature, being oppressed, commands the mind/ To suffer with the body (Lear, 2.4.100–2)

Disturbances of the mind are associated with wounded hearts and depleted physical strength. In this play, the essential link between parents and children is broken.

Although it takes him a long time to admit his partial responsibility, Lear knows that his separation from Cordelia 'wrenched [his] frame of nature' (1.4.223–7). As 'Poor Tom' raves, the obsessed Lear assumes that both of them share the same affliction, for 'nothing could have subdued nature/ To such a lowness but his unkind daughters' (3.4.65–6). Gloucester, too, admits to Lear that the grief of (apparently) losing Edgar's love 'hath crazed [his] wits' (3.4.154).

Ironically, Gloucester thinks it is 'the time's plague when madmen lead the blind' (4.1.47), just as he passes into his loving son's safe (and sane) hands and begins to find inner sight.

Knowing or losing oneself

Key Quote

Does any here know me? ... Who is it that can tell me who I am? (1.4.185, 189)

Lear's questions at this early stage of the play are rhetorical and sarcastic, designed to shame Gonerill for giving him a dressing down. The Fool sidesteps the rhetoric and tells Lear the truth – he's reduced himself to his own shadow, having lost his substance (1.4.190).

Playing the fool

Key quote

Smile you my speeches, as I were a fool? (2.2.73)

Kent is irritated by Oswald's sneering amusement at his rage but he also deliberately goads Cornwall, mimicking one of the traditional ploys of a professional Fool to get a response.

Notice how Edgar, too, steps out of his 'Poor Tom' persona to play the Fool's part for his suicidal blind father in 4.1.and 4.5, explaining, 'Why I do trifle thus with his despair/ Is done to cure it' (4.5.33–4).

Topsy-turvy

Key quote

May not an ass know when the cart draws the horse? (1.4.183)

As things go wrong in Lear's world, the Fool comments on the inversion of sensible patterns, habits, values and controls, signalling dangerous times ahead. Even Albany, not having much cause to enjoy humour, demonstrates a capacity to play the fool when Oswald arrives with news about Cordelia's army. Reporting in dismay to Gonerill, Oswald describes how Albany 'told me I had turned the wrong side out./ What most he should dislike seems pleasant to him;/ What like, offensive' (4.2.9–11).

Sight and blindness

This theme is of central significance. The play is packed with allusions to eyes, sight and blindness, ignorance and insight. The preciousness of sight is constantly explored and tested. How characters value sight is a measure of their moral worth.

Key quote

See better, Lear, and let me still remain/ The true blank of thine eye (Kent, 1.1.152–3)

Kent desperately wants to improve Lear's faulty sight in 1.1: he begs, 'let me be the spot on a target where you fix your eye and try to hit that spot every time'.

Gonerill, in contrast to Kent, blinds Lear with rhetoric: her 'eyesight' reference constitutes part of an extravagantly insincere claim about love (1.1.51). Lear says that if he ever weeps over her again he'll 'pluck out' his 'old fond eyes' (1.4.256–7). We cringe when Gonerill casually suggests they 'pluck out' Gloucester's eyes in 3.7, even more when Gloucester bravely claims he's sent the king to Dover to save Lear's 'poor old eyes' from Regan's cruel nails. Moments later, his own eyes are destroyed.

What do characters see or fail to see? Blindness can be physical, emotional, or misperception in the mind, leading to Lear's madness and Gloucester's folly. Follow the theme through the journeys of the two fathers in the play.

Key quote

I have no way and therefore want no eyes:/ I stumbled when I saw (Gloucester, 4.1.18–19)

The Gloucester plot explores how lost physical sight can lead to its replacement by insight and a sense of hopeful understanding, given the right encouragement (by Edgar). Think of the classical blind seer, Tiresias, famous for his insight.

Key quote

Get thee glass eyes/ And, like a scurvy politician, seem/ To see the things thou dost not (4.5.162–4)

Lear's journey is about the consequences of egocentricity and misperception. The cure for wrong thinking is to gain insight and discover truth. Ironically, Lear becomes more politically astute after he's given up his crown and succumbed to madness. His final mental state is more transcendental and personal than wise about the world.

Seeing the way of the world

Think about all the different ways we use images of 'seeing' in everyday language (I see what you mean, I can't see the point, I'll see to that, see that you do it, don't lose sight of your goals … the list goes on).

How reliable is physical sight as a guide to other realities? Can you see a person's nature when you look into their eyes? Lear (wrongly) thinks he can distinguish between his daughters this way: Gonerill's are 'fierce' but Regan's 'do comfort and not burn' (2.4.165–6).

Seeing and sensing

KEY QUOTE

What, art mad? A man may see how this world goes with no eyes; look with thine ears (Lear, 4.5.144–5)

When Gloucester replies to Lear's comment on seeing the world, 'I see it feelingly' (4.5.143), he provokes Lear into another feverish statement about using his other senses to discover reality. Gloucester has already thought about the same idea, when contemplating the rich man who ought to give charity but doesn't – he's someone 'that will not see/ Because he does not feel' (4.1.63–4). The idea of selective perception (only seeing what you want to see) is related to a denial of other sensory input. Gloucester and Lear both begin to explore their other natural senses of touch, smell, taste and hearing.

Most poignantly, Gloucester's wish '[m]ight I but live to see thee in my touch,/ I'd say I had eyes again' (4.1.23–4) is addressed to a son he thinks is far away. In fact, Edgar is right beside him and Gloucester will be able to embrace him before dying.

DIFFERENT INTERPRETATIONS

Different interpretations arise from different responses to a text. Over time, a text will give rise to a wide range of responses from its readers, who may come from various social or cultural groups and live in very different places and historical periods. These responses can be published in newspapers, journals and books by critics and reviewers, or they can be expressed in discussions among readers in the media, classrooms, book groups and so on. While there is no single correct reading or interpretation of a text, it is important to understand that an interpretation is more than a personal opinion – it is the justification of a point of view on the text. To present an interpretation of the text based on your point of view you must use a logical argument and support it with relevant evidence from the text.

Critical viewpoints

Whole libraries of books about the meaning of the play have been written and argued over. In the 19th century, William Hazlitt felt that *King Lear* was too big for the stage, meaning that its themes were so complex that no staging could encompass them. A. C. Bradley (*Shakespearean Tragedy*, 1905) argued that the tragedy was too 'dark' and upsetting for performance, a view many others have shared. Bradley argued strongly that the way to make sense of the suffering was to find the moral 'redemptive' lesson. John Middleton Murray in the 1950s had similar ideas, arguing that the tragic journey was through breakdown and insanity to a discovery of the Self and Divine Love. Still tending to divide along these broad lines, critics and directors have to decide whether the play shows life as bleak and meaningless or find in it hopeful and cathartic messages about the mystery of things.

Meaningful suffering and redemption in King Lear

Is there a purpose in suffering? How can madness be purgative but healing? Who needs redemption and what can be learnt? A Christian humanist approach finds strong moral values in *Lear*'s dark, cruel world by presuming that the play posits an underlying point to suffering for its characters. This kind of discussion focuses principally on Cordelia as a redeemer figure to Lear, akin to Christ redeeming sinful humanity. Edgar's spiritual guidance of Gloucester could also be included in the argument. Jonathan Miller (a psychiatrist and director of a 2004 American production of *Lear*) argues that:

> Christianity is essential to the play, although it's only there by allusion, not by explicit mention. The whole idea of gaining through loss is a specifically Christian notion – that it's only by enduring the hideous ordeal of loss that any of these people gain. (Quoted and cited in Halio, Introduction, p.60)

Cordelia's words, 'dear father, / It is thy business that I go about' (4.3.23–4) echo those of Jesus: 'Wist ye not that I must be about my

Father's business?' (Gospel of Saint Luke, 2.49).

The Gentleman tells Lear that Cordelia is saving her father from the despairing madness of his flawed human nature (brought on by Gonerill's and Regan's disobedience and ambition as daughters): 'Thou hast a daughter/ Who redeems nature from the general curse/ Which twain has brought her to' (4.5.196–8). The parallel is with Christ redeeming sinners from the consequences of Adam and Eve's original sin of disobedience to God ('twain' means two), which brought down 'the general curse' of mortality on all living things.

Lear's terrified dialogue with Cordelia betrays his mental confusion: 'You do me wrong to take me out o'th'grave' (4.6.42). Although the image seems mixed, he's either imagining that he's being brought out of his grave at Doomsday (where his soul will be judged) or that he is suffering in hell (on a 'wheel of fire'), while Cordelia bending over him seems like 'a soul in bliss'. As Cordelia calms and forgives him, Lear returns to sanity.

Read *The Book of Job* in the Old Testament, which describes a god-fearing but complacent man hit by catastrophe: he loses material possessions and children, then is afflicted with sickness. After a massive breakdown through grief, during which he curses being born and admits he is 'full of confusion', Job struggles to understand divine purpose in his suffering. There are many echoes of this imagery in *King Lear* (about speech, the senses, old age, lack of wisdom, even feet in the stocks). James I commissioned a new Bible in English, which was printed in 1611. Known as The King James Bible, it is still read for its wonderfully rich use of language. Shakespeare is thought to have been a contributor.

King Lear as endgame

Post-war Polish academic and director Jan Kott's interpretation of Shakespeare has been hugely influential. Watch Peter Brook's film version of *King Lear* (1969) to see Kott's ideas visualised. Read his discussion, 'King Lear, or Endgame', in *Shakespeare Our Contemporary* (1967, pp.100–33). Note that Brook, in his *Preface*, characterises Kott, like Shakespeare, as 'an Elizabethan', 'a poet [with] a foot in the mud, an eye on the stars and a dagger in his hand' (1967).

From the perspective of a European who had experienced life under Nazism and Stalinism, Kott's starting point in this interpretation is that there is no longer meaning in the traditional idea of 'tragedy' for modern society:

> ... fate, gods and nature have been replaced by history. History is the only framework of reference, the final authority to accept or reject the validity of human actions. It is unavoidable and realises its ultimate aims; it is objective "reason" as well as objective "progress". In this scheme of things history is a theatre with actors, but without an audience. No one watches the performance, because everyone is taking part. (Kott 1967, pp.109–10)

Kott makes an important distinction between *tragedy*, which (he argues) 'is the theatre of priests' where there's belief, hope and a sense of ultimate moral order, and *grotesque*, the theatre of clowns, which tackles the same questions as tragedy but comes to different conclusions because there are no absolutes.

> This conflict between two philosophies and two types of theatre becomes particularly acute at times of great upheaval. When established values have been overthrown, and there is no appeal to God, Nature, or History from the tortures inflicted by the cruel world, the clown becomes the central figure in the theatre. (Kott 1967, p.112)

Under such circumstances, Kott interprets Shakespeare's vision in *King Lear* as similar to his contemporary Beckett's in *Waiting for Godot* and *Endgame*. The human situation is absurd but characters still go on living. Kott argues that Elizabethans understood cruelty in *King Lear* as a 'philosophical' cruelty, as 20th-century 'new theatre' does (being neither romantic nor naturalistic). In this new theatre there are no characters, and the tragic element has been superseded by the grotesque. The grotesque is more cruel than tragedy (Kott 1967, p.103). Kott writes:

> The tragic situation becomes grotesque when both alternatives of the choice imposed are absurd, irrelevant or compromising. The hero has to play, even if there is no game. Every move is bad, but he cannot throw down his cards. To throw down the cards would also be a bad move. (Kott 1967, p.107)

In the grotesque universe, argues Kott, the Clown's position is the only viable one. Consider Kott's point when you think about Lear's madness, the Fool's desperate wit, Cordelia's silence, Edgar's antics as 'Poor Tom', and Gloucester's symbolic suicide and recovery from 'death'. They, like Beckett's characters, exist within an 'absurd mechanism' which (horrible to realise) is 'a trap set by man himself into which he has fallen' (Kott 1967, p.105).

Consider how Edward Bond's *Lear* (1971) picks up these ideas. In Peter Brook's film the Fool is played by Jack McGowran, Beckett's friend and favourite actor. Aubrey Mellor's production (Sydney Nimrod, 1984) set the play in late 20th-century war-torn Europe with 'rubble' onstage – John Bell playing Lear said in interview: 'I think the play is almost totally pessimistic and is totally atheistic. In fact, I think it mocks conventional religious beliefs of all kinds and the only virtues which exist ... are endurance, toughness, truth and loyalty.' (*Australian*, 1/2/1984, cited in Kelly 2002, Introduction).

QUESTIONS & ANSWERS

This section focuses on your own analytical writing on the text, and gives you strategies for producing high-quality responses in your coursework and exam essays.

Essay writing – an overview

An essay is a formal and serious piece of writing that presents your point of view on the text, usually in response to a given essay topic. Your 'point of view' in an essay is your interpretation of the meaning of the text's language, structure, characters, situations and events, supported by detailed analysis of textual evidence.

Analyse – don't summarise

In your essays it is important to avoid simply summarising what happens in a text:

- A **summary** is a description or paraphrase (retelling in different words) of the characters and events. For example: 'Macbeth has a horrifying vision of a dagger dripping with blood before he goes to murder King Duncan'.

- An **analysis** is an explanation of the real meaning or significance that lies 'beneath' the text's words (and images, for a film). For example: 'Macbeth's vision of a bloody dagger shows how deeply uneasy he is about the violent act he is contemplating – as well as his sense that supernatural forces are impelling him to act'.

A limited amount of summary is sometimes necessary to let your reader know which part of the text you wish to discuss. However, always keep this to a minimum and follow it immediately with your analysis (explanation) of what this part of the text is really telling us.

Plan your essay

Carefully plan your essay so that you have a clear idea of what you are going to say. The plan ensures that your ideas flow logically, that your argument remains consistent and that you stay on the topic. An essay plan should be a list of **brief dot points** – no more than half a page. It includes:

- your central argument or main contention – a concise statement (usually in a single sentence) of your overall response to the topic. See 'Analysing a sample topic' for guidelines on how to formulate a main contention.

- three or four dot points for each paragraph indicating the main idea and evidence/examples from the text. Note that in your essay you will need to *expand* on these points and *analyse* the evidence.

Structure your essay

An essay is a complete, self-contained piece of writing. It has a clear beginning (the introduction), middle (several body paragraphs) and end (the last paragraph or conclusion). It must also have a central argument that runs throughout, linking each paragraph to form a coherent whole.

See examples of introductions and conclusions in the 'Analysing a sample topic' and 'Sample answer' sections.

The introduction establishes your overall response to the topic. It includes your main contention and outlines the main evidence you will refer to in the course of the essay. Write your introduction *after* you have done a plan and *before* you write the rest of the essay.

The body paragraphs argue your case – they present evidence from the text and explain how this evidence supports your argument. Each body paragraph needs:

- a strong **topic sentence** (usually the first sentence) that states the main point being made in the paragraph

- **evidence** from the text, including some brief quotations

- **analysis** of the textual evidence explaining its significance and **explanation** of how it supports your argument

- **links back to the topic** in one or more statements, usually towards the end of the paragraph.

Connect the body paragraphs so that your discussion flows smoothly. Use some linking words and phrases like 'similarly' and 'on the other hand', though don't start every paragraph like this. Another strategy is to use a significant word from the last sentence of one paragraph in the first sentence of the next.

Use key terms from the topic – or similes for them – throughout, so the relevance of your discussion to the topic is always clear.

The conclusion ties everything together and finishes the essay. It includes strong statements that emphasise your central argument and provide a clear response to the topic.

Avoid simply restating the points made earlier in the essay – this will end on a very flat note and imply that you have run out of ideas and vocabulary. The conclusion is meant to be a logical extension of what you have written, not just a repetition or summary of it. Writing an effective conclusion can be a challenge. Try using these tips:

- Start by linking back to the final sentence of the second-last paragraph – this helps your writing to 'flow', rather than just leaping back to your main contention straight away.

- Use similes and expressions with equivalent meanings to vary your vocabulary. This enables you to reinforce your line of argument without being repetitive.

- When planning your essay, think of one or two broad statements or observations about the text's wider meaning. These should be related to the topic and your overall argument. Keep them for the conclusion, since they will give you something 'new' to say but still follow logically from your discussion. The introduction will be focused on the topic, but the conclusion can present a wider view of the text.

Essay topics

1. 'Fathers that wear rags/ Do make their children blind' sings the Fool (2.4.44–5). What do you think he means? Does the play demonstrate the truth of his statement or refute it?

2. Do you think there are enough similarities between Cordelia and the Fool to make dramatic doubling of the roles significant for an audience?

3. Discuss how several episodes in the play illustrate significantly different human ways of 'seeing'.

4. The play illustrates that Lear's 'tempest of the mind' is terrible to endure but also brings about necessary changes in him. Do you agree?

5. Is it always morally proper and justifiable to speak the truth? What are the consequences? Are there exceptions? Consider what Cordelia, Kent, Regan and Edgar decide to do.

6. Do you agree that Lear is 'more sinned against than sinning'? Does he have anything at all to answer for?

7. This play illustrates that the relationship between young and old family members is doomed to be one of conflict. Identify specific sources of conflict in the play's two families (and, if you choose, from your own experience) before arguing whether you agree or disagree.

8. Lear says, '[t]hey told me I was everything' (4.5.101). Discuss how the play explores the power of words to shape an individual's perceptions of himself or herself and of reality. Select a few characters only as your main focus.

9. In the mid-19th century, Emily Dickinson wrote 'Much Madness is divinest Sense – To a discerning Eye'. How might her definition be

applied to the kinds of madness encountered in *King Lear*?

10 How could you defend an argument that Gonerill and Regan are not necessarily as villainous as they are usually portrayed onstage?

Analysing a sample topic

The play illustrates that Lear's 'tempest of the mind' is terrible to endure but also brings about necessary changes in him. Do you agree?

This topic is asking you to focus on one character, King Lear, in relation to a central theme, the question of madness. Before you start to write, look through a synopsis and locate relevant scenes. Having reread a few scenes and considered what happens to Lear overall, you'll be able to decide to what extent you agree or disagree, and why. Remember that interesting answers don't just aim to reduce an argument's conclusion to 'either/or'.

You might recall that the topic rephrases something Lear himself describes as 'This tempest in my mind' (3.4.12). This would be a good point to pick up in your introductory sentences.

Questions to work through in your discussion:

- What has caused Lear's 'tempest'? What does *he* say? (Look in 3.4.)

- How do we know it is terrible to endure? (Find evidence in scenes, how others describe and respond to Lear, and what he says and does.)

- Does it change him? (Can you find evidence of his changing views about his daughters, his growth in self-awareness, and changing values?)

- Are changes necessary in him? Why?

The following scenes could be useful to read in preparation for your discussion. Because you don't have time to cover everything in a short essay, select a few quotes to illustrate your key points.

1.4, 1.5: The Fool goads Lear into thinking about his foolish mistake in dividing his kingdom. Lear's assumptions about his royal authority are challenged by Gonerill. He senses that he is breaking down emotionally.

2.4: Regan and Gonerill reject Lear and he feels his hysteria rising. Storm begins outside. 'O fool, I shall go mad' (2.4.279).

3.2, 3.4, 3.6: Key scenes, linking Lear's madness, the tempest within him and storm outside.

4.5: Lear's disturbing mixture of 'Reason in madness' (Edgar, 4.5.166) in his conversation with the blinded Gloucester. Lear talks about the world's corruption, philosophises about life as 'this great stage of fools' (4.5.176), and imagines killing 'son-in-laws' (4.5.178). How does he react to the Gentleman at the end of the scene? What does he think has happened?

4.6: How do his perceptions change in the scene?

5.3: Has Lear changed again? How does he respond to Cordelia's death? In Albany's view, 'He knows not what he says' (5.3.267) – do you agree?

You could quote Kent – 'The wonder is he hath endured so long' (5.3.290) – to open your final paragraph (because it gives you the chance sum up how Lear endured madness and how it changed him).

SAMPLE ANSWER

Lear says, '[t]hey told me I was everything' (4.5.101). Discuss how the play explores the power of words to shape an individual's perceptions of himself or herself and of reality. Select a few characters only as your focus.

This essay will discuss how Lear initially perceives himself through his daughters' words in 1.1, and how he learns to understand the dangerous limitations of words to evaluate life and love. From the very first scene of Shakespeare's *King Lear*, the tragedy that strikes down every major character is initiated by the power of words. As a preface to the main action in 1.1, Gloucester shares with Kent some rough speech about conceiving his children in the hearing of his illegitimate son Edmond. Gloucester's tone affects his son deeply, although Edmond masks his feelings with a show of politeness. Later, he will find ways to express his true resentment against Gloucester and his legitimate brother Edgar.

When King Lear enters, he makes his division of the kingdom between his three children dependent on how skilfully they can use words to express their love for him. Gonerill and Regan make rhetorically overblown speeches calculated to reinforce Lear's foolishly egocentric ideas about himself as a still-powerful king and a generous, loving father. Cordelia refuses to take part, for which she is disinherited. The Earl of Kent, who tries to reason with Lear in Cordelia's defence, is banished, while the King of France's words of praise for Cordelia's intrinsic virtue are ignored by Lear. The scene ends with Lear's kingdom fragmented and his court in disarray, all because of words said or unsaid.

Why do Gonerill, Regan and Cordelia say what they say in 1.1? Gonerill knows Lear's 'heart': being the eldest daughter, she accurately guesses what plausible flattery he demands and will believe as true. Her seven-line speech begins and ends by telling Lear how words aren't sufficient to express her love. The main part of her speech cynically itemises things fundamentally precious to humans, like eyesight and life, which she rhetorically devalues by comparison with her 'love' for him. Regan understands that their father 'hath ever but slenderly known himself'. Taking her cue from Gonerill, she manages to find an absurd rhetorical formula in eight lines that cancels out happiness in anything but 'your dear highness' love'. Cordelia withholds her speech because she cannot use words hypocritically to quantify love. She names the 'glib and oily art' her sisters have used to beguile their father but Lear's vanity is too crushed to allow him to perceive her meaning. Her silence challenges his habitual sense of royal authority.

Together, Gonerill and Regan tell Lear he is 'everything' and then reduce him to nothing by their actions. Lear only learns to understand how his acceptance of false words has misled his perceptions when the Fool begins to bait him in 1.4 and 1.5. When Oswald addresses Lear as 'my lady's father' (1.4.67), on Gonerill's instructions, Lear reacts to the denial of his royal title with violence, still unaware of what he gave away, by his own words, in 1.1.

After descending into hysterical madness where the logic of rational speech fails, Lear has to be helped by Kent, the Fool and 'Poor Tom' to rediscover meaning in life beyond words, in acts of simple kindness and an acceptance of bodily frailty in the storm. Finally, Lear goes to prison with Cordelia willingly, anticipating a life where they will use words innocently to sing, pray and tell old tales. His last recollection of Cordelia, the one who would not speak lies in 1.1, is when she is dead in his arms. He praises her voice – 'ever soft,/ Gentle and low, an excellent thing in woman' (5.3.246–7).

Note: You could argue this topic strongly using the characters of the sub-plot (Gloucester, Edmond and Edgar).

REFERENCES & READING

Text

Shakespeare, William 2005, *The Tragedy of King Lear*, The New Cambridge Shakespeare, Jay L. Halio (ed.), Cambridge University Press, Cambridge.

Intertexts

Bond, Edward 1971, *Lear*. Bond's *Preface* to the play, on violence, is essential reading. (Bond, Edward 1978, *Plays: Two*, Methuen.)

Smiley, Jane (novel 1991, film 1997), *A Thousand Acres*. Reworks basic outline of *King Lear* as a story of child sexual abuse, set in the American Midwest. A recent Old Vic production, directed by Peter Hall, dwelt on Lear's physical touching and kissing of his daughters in 1.1. Find Robert Smallwood's comments in *Shakespeare Survey* 51 (1998, p.248).

Further reading

Halio's reading list (pp.311–14) covers a wide range of approaches and sources discussed in his introduction, with the exception of the following:

Bullough, Geoffrey (ed.) 1973, *Narrative and Dramatic Sources of Shakespeare*, Volume VII (*Major Tragedies*), Routledge and Kegan Paul, UK & U.Columbia Press, New York. Contains all the essential likely sources for *King Lear*, including Annesley letters, Holinshed, 1605 *Leir* play text, Cordila's narrative in *The Mirror for Magistrates* (1574) and Harsnett extracts.

Delany, Paul 1995, '*King Lear* and the Decline of Feudalism', in *Materialist Shakespeare*, (ed. Ivo Kamps), Verso, London, Chapter 2, pp.20–38.

Philippa Kelly's very informative introduction to her Bell Shakespeare edition of *King Lear* (2002). She also includes extensive *Suggested Further Reading* (pp.146–52) to supplement Halio's list, with emphasis on feminist interpretations and Australian performance.

Kott, Jan 1964 (translation in paperback 1967), *Shakespeare Our Contemporary*.

Salgado, Gamini 1984, *King Lear. Text and Performance* Macmillan, Basingstoke.

Sher, Antony 1988, 'The Fool in *King Lear'*, in *Players of Shakespeare* 2, Cambridge U.P. pp.151–65. A brilliant essay by one of the most recent Fools, played as a red-nosed clown. Sher's sketches illustrate the text.

Thomas, Keith 1971, *Religion and the Decline of Magic*, Peregrine, UK (paperback 1978). Useful background to popular beliefs of Shakespeare's time, including demonic possession ('Poor Tom') and Harsnett.

Films

1969 Dir. Peter Brook (after stage production 1962).

1970 Dir. Grigori Kozintsev (discussed in Salgado 1984).

1982 Dir. Jonathan Miller BBC TV.

1983 Dir. Michael Elliott Granada TV (Olivier as Lear).

1983 *The Dresser* Dir. Peter Yates (play by Ronald Harwood). Interesting production that documents the stage Lear of Sir Donald Wolfit, who broke down at the end of his career. Harwood was Wolfit's dresser (and a Fool figure to a beloved ruined old master).

Websites

Search for 'Shakespeare King Lear' for a huge range of information. Read reviews and see photos of productions on theatre sites such as RSC, New Globe and Bell Shakespeare.

notes

CPSIA information can be obtained at www.ICGtesting.com
Printed in the USA
BVOW031030191111

276450BV00007B/31/P